BARACK OBAMA

Recent Titles in Greenwood Biographies

BARACK OBAMA

A Biography

Joann F. Price

GREENWOOD BIOGRAPHIES

GREENWOOD PRESS
WESTPORT, CONNECTICUT • LONDON

Library of Congress Cataloging-in-Publication Data

Price, Joann F.
    Barack Obama : a biography / Joann F. Price.
        p. cm. — (Greenwood biographies, ISSN 1540–4900)
    Includes bibliographical references and index.
    ISBN: 978–0–313–34488–6 (alk. paper)   1. Obama, Barack.
2. Presidential candidates—United States—Biography.   3. African
American legislators—United States—Biography.   4. Legislators—
United States—Biography.   5. United States. Congress. Senate—
Biography.   6. United States—Politics and government—2001–
7. Illinois—Politics and government—1951–   I. Title.
    E901.1.O23P75   2008
    328.73092—dc22
    [B]   2008006578

British Library Cataloguing in Publication Data is available.

Library of Congress Catalog Card Number: 2008006578

ISBN: 978–0–313–34488–6
ISSN: 1540–4900

First published in 2008

Greenwood Press, 88 Post Road West, Westport, CT 06881
An imprint of Greenwood Publishing Group, Inc.
www.greenwood.com

Printed in the United States of America

The paper used in this book complies with the
Permanent Paper Standard issued by the National
Information Standards Organization (Z39.48–1984).

10 9 8 7 6 5 4 3 2

Once again and always, to Bob. Your love and support make everything possible.

CONTENTS

Photo essay follows page 64

SERIES FOREWORD

In response to high school and public library needs, Greenwood developed this distinguished series of full-length biographies specifically for student use. Prepared by field experts and professionals, these engaging biographies are tailored for high school students who need challenging yet accessible biographies. Ideal for secondary school assignments, the length, format, and subject areas are designed to meet educators' requirements and students' interests.

Greenwood offers an extensive selection of biographies spanning all curriculum-related subject areas including social studies, the sciences, literature and the arts, history and politics, as well as popular culture, covering public figures and famous personalities from all time periods and backgrounds, both historic and contemporary, who have made an impact on American and/or world culture. Greenwood biographies were chosen based on comprehensive feedback from librarians and educators. Consideration was given to both curriculum relevance and inherent interest. The result is an intriguing mix of the well known and the unexpected, the saints and sinners from long-ago history and contemporary pop culture. Readers will find a wide array of subject choices from fascinating crime figures like Al Capone to inspiring pioneers like Margaret Mead, from the greatest minds of our time like Stephen Hawking to the most amazing success stories of our day like J. K. Rowling.

While the emphasis is on fact, not glorification, the books are meant to be fun to read. Each volume provides in-depth information about the subject's life from birth through childhood, the teen years, and adulthood.

A thorough account relates family background and education, traces personal and professional influences, and explores struggles, accomplishments, and contributions. A timeline highlights the most significant life events against a historical perspective. Bibliographies supplement the reference value of each volume.

INTRODUCTION

In no other country on earth is my story even possible.

—*Barack Obama, July 27, 2004*

On July 27, 2004, Illinois State Senator Barack Obama delivered the keynote speech at the Democratic National Convention. He said, "Tonight is a particular honor for me because, let's face it, my presence on this stage is pretty unlikely." When he finished his speech, the audience that listened with rapt attention excitedly waved their arms, hats, and signs, thrilled with what they had just heard. Afterward, those watching on television said that they had stood and cheered, many admitting they danced. Some wondered what had just happened. For many Democrats, the speech was electrifying and inspiring; for them, it was a joyful time. And those from the other side of the political aisle who watched and listened had to agree: this fresh face, this politico, unknown to nearly everyone in the country outside of his home state of Illinois, had just delivered a remarkable speech. Many asked, who is this man and where did he come from? They asked why he was selected to deliver such an important speech at the Democratic National Convention at a time described by many as a very contentious time in U.S. politics.

In the speech that evening—a speech that he wrote himself and delivered without the use of a teleprompter—Barack Obama introduced himself by first describing his father, born and raised in a small village in Kenya, and his paternal grandfather, a cook and domestic servant who, he said, had big dreams for his son. He told the immense crowd that his father, through hard work and perseverance, earned a scholarship to study in a magical place called America, which to his Kenyan countrymen was a place of freedom and opportunity. Barack told the excited crowd that July evening that his maternal grandfather worked on oil rigs and farms during the Depression and, just after Pearl Harbor, joined the army, and that his grandmother, while raising their baby, worked on a bomber assembly line during the war. He described how his grandparents moved west from Kansas, seeking opportunities, ultimately moving to Hawaii. They too, he said, had big dreams for their daughter. He said his parents met while studying at the University of Hawaii and that they shared not only an improbable love, but also an abiding faith in the possibilities of this nation. Barack said that this country's pride is based on a simple premise, summed up in the Declaration of Independence, as "the true genius of America, a faith in the simple dreams of its people, the insistence on small miracles." The speech that evening undeniably catapulted this state senator from Illinois onto the national political scene. If Americans hadn't heard of him before, they certainly knew about him now.

Barack Obama says that his story could take place only in America. He often adds that, like his parents and grandparents, anyone can achieve success through hard work and scholarship. His story is filled with good fortune, hard work, and a very good education. It is also a story of diversity of heritage that he is proud of—that is, after he came to understand and accept it.

In the United States, many political leaders throughout history have come from powerful families. For Barack Obama, this is far from the truth. His upbringing was in humble circumstances, and, while he doesn't fit any typical political mold, he is already considered by many to be one of the most dynamic figures in U.S. politics. His oratory skills, direct style, and ability to communicate are often compared with those of Abraham Lincoln, John F. Kennedy, and Robert Kennedy.

Barack Obama is truly a rising political star in the United States. With an African first name that means "blessed," his name is often mispronounced and sometimes ridiculed. However seemingly blessed, he states that he is meant to serve and to lead, and perhaps someday be president of the United States.

TIMELINE: EVENTS SIGNIFICANT TO THE LIFE OF BARACK OBAMA

1863 President Abraham Lincoln signs the Emancipation Proclamation. Barack often associates himself with President Lincoln. When he announced his candidacy for the 2008 election, he spoke in front of the Old State Capitol Building in Springfield, Illinois, where Lincoln famously declared, "A house divided against itself cannot stand."

1895 Barack's paternal grandfather, Hussein Onyango Obama, is born in Kenya.

1920 August 18—The 19th Amendment to the U.S. Constitution is ratified, giving women the right to vote.

1929 January 15—Reverend Martin Luther King Jr. is born.

1936 Barack's father, Barack Obama Sr., is born in Kenya.

1940–1945 During World War II, Barack's paternal grandfather, Hussein Onyango Obama, serves as a cook to a British captain. Stanley "Gramps" Dunham, Barack's maternal grandfather, and Madelyn "Toots" Dunham elope just prior to the attacks at Pearl Harbor on December 7, 1941. Stanley enlists in the army soon after the attacks, and Madelyn works on a bomber plane assembly line.

Barack's mother, Stanley Ann Dunham (known as Ann), is born in 1942, while her father, Stanley, is posted at an army base.

1946 August 19—President William Clinton is born.

1947 October 26—Senator Hillary Clinton is born.

1953 June 10—Senator John Edwards is born.

1959   Barack's grandparents, Stanley "Gramps" and Madelyn "Toots" Dunham, and their daughter, Stanley Ann Dunham, Barack's mother, move to Hawaii.

Ann Dunham, after being accepted by the University of Chicago, decides to enroll at the University of Hawaii. She is 18 years old.

Barack Obama Sr. leaves Kenya to attend the University of Hawaii at the age of 23.

Ann Dunham and Barack Obama Sr. meet as students at the University of Hawaii. They are soon married.

1960   September 26—The first Nixon-Kennedy debate is televised.

1961   May 4—Civil rights activists known as the Freedom Riders ride interstate busses into the segregated South; they are subsequently arrested for trespassing and unlawful assembly and are met with fire bombs and riots. Many suffer at the hands of racists.

August 4—Barack Hussein Obama is born in Hawaii.

1963   Barack Obama Sr. accepts a scholarship to attend Harvard University. Ann and Barack stay in Hawaii.

Barack Obama Sr. leaves the United States to return to Kenya. He and Ann Dunham Obama are divorced.

August 28—Reverend Martin Luther King Jr. delivers his "I have a dream" speech in Washington, DC.

November 22—President John F. Kennedy is assassinated.

1964   January 17—Michelle Robinson (Obama) is born.

July 2—President Johnson signs the Civil Rights Act into law.

October 14—Reverend Martin Luther King Jr. wins the Nobel Peace Prize for his work promoting human rights.

1965   March 7—In what later is known as Bloody Sunday, state and local police attack 600 civil rights marchers with clubs and tear gas in Selma, Alabama.

March 21—Reverend Martin Luther King Jr. leads a civil rights march from Selma, Alabama, to Montgomery, Alabama.

July 28—President Johnson commits 50,000 more troops to the conflict in Vietnam, taking the U. S. force to a total of 125,000.

August 6—President Johnson signs legislation to enact the Voting Rights Act.

1967   Ann Dunham Obama marries Lolo Soetoro, an Indonesian student attending the University of Hawaii. Lolo leaves Hawaii for Indonesia; Ann makes plans for her and Barack to follow.

Barack leaves Hawaii to move to Jakarta, Indonesia, with his mother and his stepfather. Barack's half sister Maya is born in Indonesia.

1968   April 4—Reverend Martin Luther King Jr. is assassinated. June 6—Senator Robert F. Kennedy is assassinated.

August 28—Antiwar protestors demonstrate at the Democratic convention in Chicago.

1969   November 16—An estimated 250,000 people gather in Washington, D.C., to protest the Vietnam War.[1]

1970   June 22—President Richard Nixon signs an extension of the Voting Rights Act that lowers the voting age to 18. Known as the 26th Amendment to the Constitution, it is ratified on July 1, 1971.

1971   Barack leaves Indonesia to live with his grandparents in Hawaii. Ann and Barack's half sister Maya stay in Indonesia. He is 10 years old.

Fall—As a fifth grader, Barack attends the prestigious prep school Punahou Academy.

Barack Obama Sr., recuperating from a serious car accident, visits Barack in Hawaii. Barack was two when his father left Hawaii for Harvard Law School.

1979   Barack's paternal grandfather, Hussein Onyango Obama, dies in Kenya.

Barack graduates from Punahou Academy. After being accepted by several schools, he enrolls in Occidental College in Los Angeles.

Having always been called Barry by friends and family, he is now called Barack, which means "blessed" in Arabic.

1980   As a sophomore, Barack gets involved with a South African divestment campaign on campus and gives his first speech at a rally.

1981   August—Barack, now 20 years old, transfers from Occidental College to Columbia University in New York City.

1982   Barack receives a call from Nairobi, Kenya. It is his Aunt Jane, whom he has never met, telling him that his father has been killed in a car accident. Barack is 21 years old.

1983   Barack graduates from Columbia University. He takes a job in New York as a research assistant at a consulting firm.

1984   President Ronald Reagan signs a policy directive designed to combat international terrorism. This gives the United States the power to launch preventive and retaliatory strikes against foreign terrorists.[2]

1985   Barack accepts a position as a community organizer and moves to Chicago. During his three years on the job, his half sister Auma visits him and he learns about his father and the family in Kenya.

1988   February—Barack is accepted by Harvard Law School. Prior to attending classes in the fall, he makes his first trip to Kenya.
        Fall—At 27 years of age, Barack begins law school.

1989   Summer—Barack returns to Chicago as an intern at a law firm. He meets Michelle Robinson, his future wife, who is assigned as his mentor. She graduated from Harvard Law School in 1988.

1990   During his second year of law school, Barack is elected president of the prestigious *Harvard Law Review*. He is the first African American to be elected to the position in the *Review*'s 104-year history.

1991   Barack graduates magna cum laude from Harvard Law School. After being heavily recruited by law firms across the nation, he returns to Chicago to practice civil rights law.

1992   Barack and Michelle Robinson are married. Barack and Michelle visited Kenya prior to their marriage to meet Barack's family. They move to Hyde Park, a suburb on Chicago's South Side.
        Barack's grandfather Stanley Dunham dies prior to Barack and Michelle's marriage.
        Barack becomes the director of Illinois Project Vote, helping to register nearly 50,000 voters.
        William Jefferson Clinton is elected president of the United States.

1993   Barack goes to work at a public interest law firm to work on civil rights, employment discrimination, fair housing, and voting rights.
        Barack is named in *Crain's* magazine's list of "40 under 40" outstanding young leaders in the city of Chicago.
        Barack joins the faculty of University of Chicago Law School as a senior lecturer, teaching constitutional law.

Michelle Obama joins the Chicago Office of Public Allies, a program that assists young people to find employment in public service.

February 26—A bomb explodes in the World Trade Center in New York.

1995   Barack publishes his first book, *Dreams from My Father*.

1996   Barack is elected to the Illinois State Senate as a Democrat representing the Illinois 13th legislative district.

1997   January—State Senator Barack Obama arrives in Springfield, Illinois, to serve his constituency from the South Side of Chicago.

1998   Barack and Michelle's first daughter, Malia, is born.

2000   Barack enters the race for the U.S. House of Representatives against the four-term incumbent Bobby Rush. He loses by a two-to-one margin.

George W. Bush is elected president.

2001   Barack and Michelle's second daughter, Sasha, is born.

September 11—Often referred to as 9/11, al Qaeda launches a series of coordinated suicide attacks in New York, Washington, DC, and Pennsylvania.

2002   Midyear—Barack announces to his friends his decision to run for the U.S. Senate.

Fall—A majority of Americans are convinced that Saddam Hussein has weapons of mass destruction and is personally involved in the 9/11 attacks.

October—The Senate votes to give President George W. Bush the power to go to war in Iraq.

October 2—Barack speaks to a crowd of antiwar activists, stating his opposition to the war.

2004   March 16—Barack wins the primary election for the U.S. Senate with 53 percent of the vote. He would face Republican Alan Keyes in the general election.

July 27—Barack delivers the keynote speech at the Democratic National Convention in Boston, Massachusetts. The speech lasts approximately 15 minutes.

With a margin of victory of 70 percent over Alan Keyes's 27 percent, Barack is elected to the U.S. Senate. He is the only African American in the U.S. Senate and the fifth African American in U.S. history.

December—Barack signs a contract for three more books, including a children's book to be written with Michelle.

2005   January 4—Barack is sworn in as a member of the 109th Congress of the United States.

Shortly after his swearing in as the junior senator from Illinois, Barack and his team begin making plans for a 15-day trip to Africa.

Upon his return from Africa, plans begin in earnest about a run for the presidency in the 2008 election.

Barack is one of two freshmen senators on the powerful Senate Foreign Relations Committee.

August—Barack travels to Russia with Republican Senator Richard Lugar and others to inspect nuclear and biological weapons sites. He then cosponsors a bill that will reduce the stockpiles of these types of weapons.

August—Hurricane Katrina devastates the southern coastal regions of the United States. Barack speaks out about poverty issues and the government's handling of the devastation.

During his first two years as a senator, Barack travels around the world, studying nuclear proliferation, AIDS, and violence in the Middle East. Speculation continues about whether he is considering a presidential run.

2006   Barack publishes his second book, *The Audacity of Hope: Thoughts on Reclaiming the American Dream.*

October 22—Barack appears on the NBC television show *Meet the Press,* where he tells commentator Tim Russert that it is fair to say he is thinking about running for president in 2008.

October 23—Barack appears on the cover of *Time* magazine in an article entitled "Why Barack Obama Could Be the Next President."

November—After the Democrats take control of Congress in the general election, discussions about Barack's presidential bid take on more urgency, with Michelle Obama's opinion the key to the decision on whether he will run.

December—Michelle determines she is on board with her husband running for president.

December—Barack visits New Hampshire, an early presidential primary state, and tells an audience that the media describe as "rock-star size" that America is ready to turn a page and a new generation is prepared to lead.

2007   January—Barack tells *U.S. News & World Report* that he believes there is a great hunger for change in America.

January—Barack takes another step in a presidential bid by posting a message on his Web site and sending an e-mail message to his Web site subscribers that he is forming a presidential exploratory committee. He tells his supporters and subscribers that the decision to run for the presidency is a profound one and that he wants to be sure whatever decision he makes is right for him, his family, and the country.

January—Barack says he will tell his friends, neighbors, and Americans by February 10 what his plans are regarding running for president.

February 10—On a frigid day in Springfield, Illinois, in front of a crowd estimated to be at least 10,000 people, Barack announces that he is running for president of the United States.

March—A *USA Today*/Gallup Poll finds that 1 in 10 say they wouldn't vote for a woman or Hispanic, and 1 in 20 say they wouldn't vote for a black, Jewish, or Catholic candidate.[3]

March—Barack announces his campaign has raised more than 100,000 donations totaling at least $25 million; $6.9 million is generated through Internet donations.[4]

March—Barack speaks at the Brown Chapel AME church in Selma, Alabama, on the anniversary of Bloody Sunday. He tells the assembly that the event in 1965, when state and local police attacked 600 civil rights marchers with clubs and tear gas, enabled his parents, a mixed-race couple, to marry.

April—Many in the media cast Barack as a candidate who has refused money from Washington lobbyists and who uses the Internet to garner support and contributions.

April—Barack announces the Five Initiatives: bringing the Iraq war to an end, modernizing the military, stopping the spread of weapons of mass destruction, rebuilding alliances and partnerships, and investing in our common humanity.

May—Barack is placed under Secret Service protection, the earliest ever for a U.S. presidential candidate.

May—Barack is selected by *Time* magazine as one of the world's most influential people.

July—A *Newsweek* magazine poll finds that race is no longer the barrier it once was in electing a president. A clear majority, 59 percent, say that the country is ready to elect an African American president, up from 37 percent at the start of the decade.[5]

December—A report by the Pew Research Center finds that "fewer people are making judgments about candidates based solely, or even mostly, on race itself."[6]

2008 Barack is consistently considered to be a front-runner in national and state polls, along with Senator Hillary Clinton and Senator John Edwards.

January 3—Barack's first test comes at the Iowa caucus. He sails to victory with 38 percent of the state delegate vote in a contest that features a record turnout of at least 239,000. The win gives his presidential campaign an early and extremely important boost.[7]

January 8—In the first presidential primary for the 2008 election, New Hampshire's, the second test for his candidacy, with polls suggesting an enormous victory, Barack takes second place behind Senator Hillary Clinton, with 36 percent of the vote to Clinton's 39 percent.[8]

January 15—Michigan holds its primary, but the votes do not count as the Democratic National Party stripped the state of its delegates for violating Party rules by holding the primary too early. Barack had withdrawn his name from the ballot; Hillary's name remained, but no delegates are awarded.

January 19—The campaigns move to Nevada for the state's caucus. More than 117,000 vote, compared to the 9,000 that voted in 2004.[9] Hillary wins the contest with 51 percent of the vote to Barack's 45 percent.[10]

January 25—South Carolina holds its primary. Voters come out in droves to hear Barack's message. Barack wins 55 percent of the vote, doubling Hillary's share.[11]

January 29—Florida holds its primary. As in the Michigan primary the votes do not count and the Democratic National Party strips the delegates for violating Party rules. Both Barack and Hillary had agreed not to campaign in the state, however Hillary had held fund-raising events there. No delegates are awarded.

February 5—Known as Super Tuesday, 22 states hold either a primary or a caucus. In all, there are more than

2,000 delegates at stake including the delegate-rich states of California with 441, Illinois with 185, and New York with 281. When all the votes are counted, Barack wins 13 individual states, including his home state of Illinois; Hillary wins 8 states, including her adopted home state of New York. The popular vote from Super Tuesday makes it a very close race. Clinton wins 7,427,700 popular votes, or 50.20 percent; Obama wins 7,369,709 popular votes, or 49.80 percent.[12]

February 9—The states of Nebraska, Washington, Louisiana, and the Virgin Islands hold contests where excitement is high and the turnout is record-breaking. With a total of 203 delegates at stake, Barack wins all four states.

February 10—Maine holds its caucus with 34 delegates at stake. Barack wins 59 percent of the vote; Hillary wins 40 percent.[13]

February 12—Known as the Potomac Primaries, Washington, D.C., Maryland, and Virginia hold their primaries for a total of 240 delegates. Barack sweeps all three states winning 75 percent of the vote to Hillary's 24 percent in Washington, D.C.; in Maryland, Barack wins 60 percent to Hillary's 37 percent; and in Virginia, Barack wins 64 percent to Hillary's 35 percent.[14]

February 19—The campaigns move to Wisconsin for a primary with 121 delegates at stake, and to Hawaii with 20 delegates. To no one's surprise, Barack carries Hawaii with 76 percent of the vote. In Wisconsin, Barack wins 58 percent to Hillary's 41 percent.[15]

March 4—Another Tuesday rich with delegates: Texas, Ohio, Vermont, and Rhode Island hold contests. Hillary is favored to win in Texas with 193 delegates and Ohio with 141 delegates. When all votes are counted, Barack wins Vermont by 30 points, and Hillary wins the other three states.[16]

March 8—With 18 total delegates, Wyoming holds its primary. Barack wins 61 percent to Hillary's 38 percent.[17]

March 11—Mississippi holds its primary with 40 delegates at stake. Barack wins 61 percent to Hillary's 37 percent.[18] Both campaigns prepare for the next primary, in Pennsylvania on April 22, 2008, where they will vie for 188 delegates. The primary calendar includes contests in Guam on May 3, Indiana and North Carolina on May 6, West

Virginia on May 13, Kentucky and Oregon on May 20, Puerto Rico on June 1, and Montana and South Dakota on June 3, 2008.

March 18—At the National Constitution Center in Philadelphia, Pennsylvania, Barack speaks for nearly 40 minutes about race and racial rhetoric. Afterwards, many compare it to Dr. Martin Luther King's "I Have a Dream" speech.

NOTES

1. Leonard Spinrad and Thelma Spinrad, *On This Day in History* (Paramus, NJ: Prentice Hall, 1999), 328.

2. Ibid., 105–106.

3. Susan Page, "2008 Race Has the Face of a Changing America," *USA Today,* March 12, 2007.

4. Jeremy Pelofsky, "Sen. Obama Nears Clinton in Campaign Money Race," *Reuters,* April 4, 2007.

5. "Black and White," *Newsweek,* July 8, 2007.

6. Gary Younge, "The Obama Effect," *The Nation,* December 31, 2007.

7. Greg Giroux, "Obama and Huckabee Score Upsets in Iowa," *CQ Today,* January 4, 2008.

8. Michael Duffy, "Obama Moves On, Without a Bounce," *Time,* January 9, 2008.

9. Robin Toner, "High Enthusiasm Propels Democrats," *New York Times,* January 29, 2008, A.1.

10. "Election Guide 2008," *New York Times,* February 13, 2008, http://politics.nytimes.com/election-guide/2008/results/votes/index.html.

11. Bob Benenson and Marie Horrigan, "Obama Wins Convincingly in South Carolina as Rivals Look Ahead," *CQ Today Online,* January 27, 2008. http://www.cqpolitics.com.

12. Patrick Healy, "Obama and Clinton Brace for Long Run," *New York Times,* February 7, 2008, A.1.

13. "Election Guide 2008," *New York Times,* February 13, 2008, http://politics.nytimes.com/election-guide/2008/results/votes/index.html.

14. Ibid.

15. "Election Guide 2008," *New York Times,* March 18, 2008, http://politics.nytimes.com/election-guide/2008/results/votes/index.html.

16. Ibid.

17. Ibid.

18. Ibid.

Chapter 1

FAMILY HISTORY

What's interesting is how deeply American I feel, considering this exotic background. Some of it is the Midwestern roots of my grandparents, my mother, and the values that they reflect. But some of it is also a deep abiding sense that what is quintessentially American, is all these different threads coming together to make a single quilt. And I feel very much like I'm one of those threads that belong in this quilt, that I'm a product of all these different forces, black, white, Asian, Hispanic, Native American. That, somehow, all this amalgam is part of who I am, and that's part of the reason I love this country so much.[1]

HUSSEIN ONYANGO OBAMA, BARACK OBAMA'S PATERNAL GRANDFATHER; AKUMA OBAMA, BARACK OBAMA'S PATERNAL GRANDMOTHER; GRANNY, HUSSEIN ONYANGO OBAMA'S THIRD WIFE

In 1988, before moving to Boston to attend Harvard Law School, Barack made an important trip to Kenya. He felt he needed a break from his two and a half years as a community organizer in Chicago; and, as he later answered his half brother Bernard when asked why he had finally come home, he said that he wasn't sure why, but something had told him it was time. What he found in Africa was more than just a simple connection to family. Rather, it was a pilgrimage for this young man who grew up conflicted by his mixed race and by his father's absence that came so early in his life.

After traveling through Europe for three weeks, intending to see places he'd always heard about but had never seen, he realized he'd made a mistake in touring there first. Europe wasn't a part of his heritage, and he felt he was living as if he were someone else, lending an incompleteness to his own history. He also thought spending time in Europe before his trip to Africa might be an attempt to delay coming to terms with his father. When Barack was two, his father returned to Africa, leaving him and his mother in Hawaii. He hadn't seen his father since he was 10 years old.

With some relief at leaving Europe, and with more than a little nervousness at the prospect of facing a family history he knew very little about, he flew from London to Nairobi, Kenya. Landing at the Kenyatta International Airport, his sister and aunt warmly greeted him and welcomed him home. His Aunt Zeituni told his half sister Auma, "You take good care of Barry now. Make sure he doesn't get lost again." Barack was confused by this greeting, and Auma explained that this was a common expression referring to someone who hasn't been seen for a while or to someone who has left and not been seen again; they've been lost, she said, even if people know where they are.[2] For Barack, known as Barry to his family and friends until later in his life, a pilgrimage had begun.

While in Kenya, Barack met members of his African family. He met his half sisters, half brothers, aunts, and cousins; he learned about his father and grandfather and what it meant to be an Obama—as many throughout Kenya remembered Barack Sr. and Hussein Obama, Barack's grandfather. To know more about his grandfather Hussein, Barack and his aunts, sister, and brothers boarded a train to visit Granny, the third wife of Hussein Obama. The train, originally built by the British beginning in 1895, was part of a 600-mile rail line from the city of Mombasa on the Indian Ocean to the eastern shores of Lake Victoria. This trip was an important part of Barack's pilgrimage in Africa, because it would take him to what is known as "Home Squared," the ancestral family home. Barack's half sister Auma and her brother Roy, Barack's half brother, had visited there many times. Auma told Barack that he would love Granny, adding that she had a wonderful sense of humor, something she said Granny needed after living with "The Terror," her name for their grandfather. She said they called their grandfather that because he was so mean. Roy added that their grandfather would make them sit at the table for dinner, serve the food on china, like an Englishman, and if someone said the wrong thing or used the wrong fork, he would hit them on the head with his stick. Barack's Aunt Zeituni assured Barack that she had many good memories about her father; he was strict, yes, but he was well respected.

Barack's grandfather's compound, in the village of Alego, was one of the largest in the area. He was known to be an excellent farmer, and it was said he could make anything grow. Aunt Zeituni said that Hussein Obama had worked for the British during World War II, serving a captain in the British army. After working as a cook for many years, he learned their farming techniques and applied them to his own land.

Auma suggested that if there were difficulties within the Obama family, they all seemed to stem from Grandfather Hussein, saying he was the only person their father, Barack Sr., feared. To Barack, this seemed right somehow, and if he could learn more, fit the pieces of the story together, he thought everything might fall into place.[3]

Arriving at the village where Granny lived, Barack first met his father's two brothers, Yusuf and Sayid. Sayid, his father's youngest brother, said he had heard many great things about his nephew and warmly welcomed him. There, in a compound with a low, rectangular house with a corrugated-iron roof and concrete walls and bougainvillea with red, pink, and yellow flowers, a few chickens, and two cows beneath a mango tree, was what he came to know as "Home Squared." A large woman with a scarf on her head and wearing a flowered skirt came out of the main house. She had sparkling eyes and a face like his Uncle Sayid's. "Halo!" she said. Speaking in Luo, her African language, she said she had dreamed about the day when she would finally meet the son of her son and that his coming had brought her great happiness. Welcoming him home, she gave Barack a hug and led him into the house, where there were pictures of Barack's father, his Harvard diploma, a picture of his grandfather, and a picture of another grandmother, Akuma, his father's mother. After enjoying tea, Barack visited two graves at the edge of a cornfield. One had a plaque for his grandfather; the other was covered with tiles, but there was no plaque. Roy, Barack's half brother, explained that for six years, there had been nothing to note who was buried there.

For the rest of the day, Barack was immersed in the daily life of Granny's compound and the nearby village. Remembering each part of the day, he said, "It wasn't simply joy that I felt in each of these moments. Rather, it was a sense that everything I was doing, every touch and breath and word, carried the full weight of my life; that a circle was beginning to close, so that I might finally recognize myself as I was, here, now, in one place."[4]

It was in Granny's compound—where his grandfather had farmed and where members of his family still worked the land—where he heard the stories. One day, in the shade of a mango tree, Barack asked Granny to start at the beginning and tell him about his family. He said that, as Granny began to speak, he heard all his family's voices run together, the sounds of three generations were like a stream and his questions like rocks in the water.[5] Granny told Barack that his great-great grandfather cleared his own land and became prosperous, with many cattle and goats. She said he had four wives and many children, one of which was Barack's grandfather. Although the children didn't attend school, they learned from their parents and elders of the tribe; the men learned how to herd and hunt, and the women learned how to farm and cook. The legend of his grandfather, Granny said, was that he was restless and would wander off for days; he was an herbalist, learning about plants that could cure and heal. When he was still a boy, white men came to the area for the first time, and Onyango was curious about them. He left the farm for a few months, and when he returned he was wearing clothes like the white men—pants, shirts, and shoes on his feet, which made his family suspicious of him. He was banished by his own father and soon left, returning to the town of Kisumu, where he had lived and worked for the white people who had settled there. He learned to read and write and learned about land titles and accounting. His skills made him valuable to the British. Because Africans in those days couldn't ride the train, he walked to Nairobi, a two-week trip on foot, and began to work in a British household. He prospered in his job, which included preparing food and organizing the household. He became popular among his employers and was able to save his wages to buy land and cattle in Kendu, not far from Granny's land.

On his land, Onyango built a hut, but it wasn't like the traditional huts nearby. Instead, it was kept spotlessly clean, and he insisted that people entering remove their shoes. As well, he ate his meals at a table, using a knife and fork. He insisted that the food he ate be washed, and he bathed and washed his clothes every night. He was very strict about his property, but if asked, he would gladly give someone food, clothing, or money. If someone took something without asking, however, he became very angry. His manners were considered strange by his neighbors. By this time, he hadn't married, and this too was unusual. At one point, he decided he needed to marry; however, because of his high housekeeping standards, no woman could maintain his home as he demanded. After several attempts at marriage, and after losing the precious dowries paid for women to be his wife, he found a woman who could live with him. After a few years, it was discovered that she could not bear children, and even though this was typically grounds for divorce among the Luo tribe, she was allowed to remain in the compound, living in a hut that was built for her. Barack's grandfather was still living and working in Nairobi at this time, but he often returned to Kendu to visit his land. He decided he needed a second wife and returned to Kendu to inquire about the women in the village. He chose a young girl named Akumu, who was known for her great beauty. They had three children; the second child was Barack's father. Later, he married again; his third wife was Granny, who, at 16, married Onyango and lived in Nairobi with him. Akumu, living with her children in Kendu, was very unhappy, and her spirit, according to Granny, was rebellious. She found her husband too demanding. He was strict with the housekeeping and with child rearing. Life became easier for his second wife when, at the start of World War II, Onyango went overseas with the British captain, as his cook. He traveled with the British forces for three years and, upon his return, brought home a gramophone and a picture of a woman he said he had married in Burma.

By the age of 50, Onyango decided to leave the employ of the British and moved to Alego, the land of his grandfather, leaving his farm in the village of Kendu. Because he had studied British techniques and learned modern farming while in Nairobi, he put these methods to work on land that was mostly African bush. In less than a year, Onyango had enough crops to market. His grandfather planted the trees that Barack saw on Granny's land. He built huts for his wives and children and built an oven for baking bread and cakes. He played music at night and provided beds and mosquito nets for the children. He taught his neighbors about farming and medicines and was well respected by them. When Barack Sr. was eight, his mother decided to leave her husband, leaving the children in Granny's care. She had tried to leave several times before, always returning to her family home; always Onyango had demanded that she return. This time, Onyango at first decided to let her go. However, because Granny had two children of her own, he went to Akumu's family and demanded that his second wife be returned to care for their children. This time, the family refused because they had already accepted a dowry from another man whom Akumu had married; the two had left for Tanganyika. There was nothing Onyango could do, and he told his third wife she was now the mother of all of his children. Sarah, Barack Sr.'s older sister, resented her father and remained loyal to her mother. Barack Sr. had a different view and told everyone Granny was his mother. Granny told Barack that his grandfather continued to be very strict with his children. He did not allow them to play outside the compound, mostly because he felt the other children were dirty and ill mannered. She added that when her husband was away, she would let them play as they wished, believing they needed to be children.

By the time Barack Sr. was in his teens, life in Kenya was rapidly changing. Many Africans had fought in the war, and when they returned to their homeland, they were eager to use what they learned as fighters;

they were no longer satisfied with white rule. Many young Africans were influenced by discussions about independence. Barack's grandfather was skeptical that talk about independence would lead to anything, and he thought Africans could never win against a white man's army. He told his son, "How can the African defeat the white man when he cannot even make his own bicycle?" He said that the African could never win against the white man because the black man wanted to work only with his own family or clan, while all white men worked to increase their power. He said that white men worked together and nation and business were important to them. He said that white men follow their leaders and do not question orders, but black men think they know what is better for them. That is why, he said, the black man will always lose.[6] Despite these opinions, government authorities detained Onyango, declaring him a subversive and a supporter of those demanding independence. He was placed in a detention camp and was later found innocent. When he returned home, after being in the camp for six months, he was very thin and had difficulty walking. He was ashamed of his appearance and his diminished capacity, and, from that time on, he appeared to be an old man, far from the vital man he had been prior to the false accusation.

Granny told Barack that what his grandfather respected was strength and discipline. And, despite learning many of the white man's ways, he remained strict about his Luo traditions, which included respect for elders and for authority and order and custom in all his affairs. She thought that was why he had rejected the Christian religion, saying that, for a brief time, he had converted to Christianity and even changed his name to Johnson. He couldn't understand the ideas of mercy toward enemies, she said, and then had converted to Islam, thinking its practices conformed more closely to his beliefs.[7]

After several years, Barack Sr. moved away from his father's home to work in Mombassa. He later applied to universities in the United States. Onyango supported his son's desire to study abroad but had little money to support his efforts. Barack Sr. was accepted at the University of Hawaii, and, through a scholarship and monies he received from benefactors, the funds were raised for him to leave Africa. When he met Ann Dunham, Barack's mother, he proposed marriage. Onyango disapproved of the marriage, feeling his son was not acting responsibly. He wrote to Barack Sr., "How can you marry this white woman when you have responsibilities at home? Will this woman return with you and live as a Luo woman? . . . Let the girl's father come to my hut and discuss the situation properly. For this is the affairs of elders, not children." He also wrote to Barack's grandfather, Stanley Dunham, and said the same things.[8] Onyango threatened to have his son's visa revoked. Despite his father's opinions, the marriage took place. When Barack Sr. returned to Kenya without his wife and young son, Onyango wasn't surprised and knew his predictions had come true. When Onyango died, Barack Sr. returned to his father's home to make arrangements for his burial.

At the end of Granny's story, told in the shade of the mango tree, Barack asked her if there was anything left of his grandfather's belongings. Sorting through the contents of an old trunk, he found a rust-colored book about the size of a passport. The cover of the small book said: *Domestic Servant's Pocket Register, Issued under the Authority of the Registration of Domestic Servant's Ordinance, 1928, Colony and Protectorate of Kenya.* Inside were his grandfather's left and right thumbprints. A preamble inside the book explained that the object of the book was to present a record of employment and to protect employers against the employment of those who were deemed unsuitable for work. The little book defined the term *servant* and stated that the book was to be carried by servants or they would be subject to fines or imprisonment if they were found without the document. Barack's grandfather's name, Hussein II Onyango, his ordinance number, race, place of residence, sex, age, height, and physical attributes were all listed. His employment history was listed as well as a review of his performance in each capacity. Along with the little book was a stack of application-for-admission letters from Barack's father, all addressed to universities in the United States. To Barack, this was his inheritance, the documents about his grandfather, some letters describing his father, and all the stories he heard on his pilgrimage to Kenya.

STANLEY DUNHAM, KNOWN AS GRAMPS, AND MADELYN "TOOTS" DUNHAM—BARACK OBAMA'S MATERNAL GRANDPARENTS

Barack Obama writes affectionately about his maternal grandparents throughout his book *Dreams from My Father.* From the time he was born until he left for college in California, Barack frequently lived with his mother's parents, and they had an immeasurable influence on him. Madelyn, or Toots, a derivation of Tutu, the Hawaiian name for grandparent, grew up in Kansas. Her heritage included Cherokee and Scottish and English ancestors who homesteaded on the Kansas prairie. Stanley also grew up in Kansas, in a town less than 20 miles from Madelyn. In his book, Barack writes that they recalled their childhoods in small-town Depression-era America, complete with Fourth of July parades, fireflies, dust storms, hailstorms, and classrooms filled with farm boys.[9] They frequently spoke about respectability, saying that you didn't have to be rich to be respectable. Madelyn's family, he wrote, were hardworking, decent people. Her father had a job throughout the Depression. Her mother, a teacher prior to having a family, kept the home spotless and ordered books through the mail. Stanley's parents were Baptists, and his mother committed suicide when Stanley was eight years old. Known to be a bit wild in his youth, Stanley was thrown out of high school for punching the principal in the nose. For the next three years, he did odd jobs and often rode the rail lines around the country. Winding up in Wichita, Kansas, he met Madelyn, after she moved there with her family. Her parents didn't approve of their courtship. Barack describes his grandfather in the days before World War II as cutting a dashing figure, wearing baggy pants and a starched undershirt and a brimmed hat cocked back on his head. He describes his grandmother as a smart-talking girl with too much red lipstick, dyed blond hair, and legs that could model hosiery for the department store.[10] Madelyn and Stanley eloped just prior to the attack at Pearl Harbor. Stanley enlisted in the army and, while he was posted at an army base, Barack's mother Ann was born. Madelyn went to work on a bomber plane assembly line. After the war, the family moved to California, where Stanley enrolled at the University of California, Berkeley, using the benefits of the GI bill. After a time, Stanley realized that being in a classroom wasn't right for him, and the family moved back to Kansas, then to Texas, and finally to Seattle, where Stanley worked as a furniture salesman and where Ann finished high school. Ann was offered early admission to the University of Chicago; however, Stanley forbade her to go, believing she was too young to live on her own.

At about this same time, the manager of the furniture company mentioned that a new store was about to open in Honolulu, Hawaii. He said that the opportunities seemed endless there, because statehood was imminent. The Dunhams sold their home in Seattle and moved again. Stanley worked as a furniture salesman, and Madelyn began working as a secretary at a local bank. Eventually, she became the first woman vice president at the bank.

Barack describes the move to Hawaii as part of his grandfather's perpetual search for a new beginning. By the time they moved, Stanley's character would be fully formed, with a generosity and eagerness to please and a mix of sophistication and provincialism. He writes that his grandfather was typical of men of his generation—men who embraced freedom and individualism and who were both dangerous and promising. Stanley wrote poetry, listened to jazz music, and counted as friends many Jewish people he met in the furniture business. His grandmother, in contrast, was skeptical by nature, with a stubborn independence, and deeply private and pragmatic. To Barack, they appeared to be of a liberal bent, although, he writes, their beliefs were never like a firm ideology. When his mother came home from the University of Hawaii, telling her parents that she met a man from Kenya, Africa, named Barack, their first impulse was to invite him over for dinner.[11]

After Barack was born, his grandparents loved him fiercely and fearlessly. They were proud of him, and his mixed parentage never seemed to be an issue for them. They encouraged him, disciplined him, and saw that he received his education and did his best in school. While Barack's mother remained in Indonesia after sending her son back to Hawaii to attend school and when she later returned to Indonesia to further her anthropology studies, Barack lived with Stanley and Toots. Although she was more reserved than Stanley, Toots's love for her grandson was never in question. She always encouraged Barack and enjoyed it when his friends came over to play or, later, to just hang out. Neil Abercrombie, a Democratic congressman from Hawaii and a close friend of Ann and Barack Sr. at the University of Hawaii, said he would frequently see Stanley and Barack about town and added, "Stanley loved that little boy. In the absence of his father, there was not a kinder, more understanding man than Stanley Dunham. He was loving and generous."[12]

BARACK OBAMA SENIOR, BARACK OBAMA'S FATHER

A few months after Barack's 21st birthday, when he was living in New York, a stranger called. It was his Aunt Jane, calling from Nairobi to tell Barack that his father had been killed in a car accident. She asked that he call his uncle in Boston and relay the news. Telling him she would try to call again, the line went dead. The news about a father he hadn't seen since he was 10, the father who had returned to Africa in 1963 when Barack was only 2 years old, wasn't easily processed. Now, at 21 years of age, he heard from an aunt he didn't know that his father, who was somewhat more a myth than a man, was dead.

Barack writes in his book *Dreams from My Father* that, at the time of his father's death, he really only knew him from the stories he had heard from his mother and grandparents. They each had their favorites that young Barack heard many times. His grandmother seemed to have a "gentler portrait" of Barack Sr. Barack's mother said that his father could be a bit domineering and that he was an honest person and sometimes uncompromising. She told him the story of his father accepting his Phi Beta

Kappa key in his favorite outfit of jeans and an old knit leopard-print shirt. No one had said it was a big honor, and when he found everyone at the ceremony dressed in tuxedos, he was, for the first and only time in her memory, embarrassed. Barack's grandfather said that Barack Sr. could handle just about any situation, a quality that made everyone like him. Barack's grandfather said that one thing Barack could learn from his father was confidence, which he believed was the secret to a man's success.[13] The stories were often told in the evenings, and then stories about his father would be put away, to be brought up again at a later time. Later in life, Barack learned more about his father, the man he and his half sister Auma called the "old man," from the stories he heard on his first trip to Kenya.

Barack's father was a Kenyan, of the Luo tribe, born near Lake Victoria in a village called Alego. His mother Akumu, his father's second wife, left the household when Barack Sr. was nine, leaving her first two children to be raised by his father's third wife, known to her extended family as Granny, and taking her third child, an infant, with her. Granny described Barack Sr. as mischievous, appearing to be obedient in front of his father, but, outside of his father's view, he usually did what he pleased. Even though he behaved badly sometimes, he was also very clever. At a very early age, he learned his alphabet and numbers.

As a young man, Barack Sr. tended his father's goats and attended the local mission school that had been set up by the British. Learning came very easily to him, and he told his father he could not study there because he already knew everything the instructor had to teach him. He was sent to another school, and even there he knew all the answers and corrected his teacher. He soon became bored with school and would sometimes stop going altogether. He would find a classmate to give him the lessons and would learn everything he needed to know for the exam. He was almost always first in his class. This pleased his father, because, to him, knowledge was the source of white man's power, and he wanted to make sure his son was as educated as any white man. Life in Kenya was changing by the time Barack Sr. was a teenager. Many Africans had fought in World War II, and when they returned home, they weren't satisfied with living under the white man's rule. There was talk of independence from the British. Barack Sr. was influenced by all the talk, and when he returned home from school he often talked about what he had seen. Although his father, Onyango, agreed with many of the demands, he was skeptical of any sort of independence. He thought Africans could never win against the white man's army. He said that the black man only wanted to work with his own family or clan, while all the white men worked to increase their power. "The white man alone is like an ant. He can be easily crushed . . .

the white man works together. His nation, his business—these things are more important to him . . . he will follow his leaders and not question order. Black men are not like this. Even the most foolish black man thinks he knows better . . . that is why the black man will always lose."[14] Despite these views, Onyango was thought to be a subversive and spent time in a detention camp. Even though he was later found innocent, he never fully recovered from the experience.

While his father was in a detention camp, Barack Sr. was away at school, some 50 miles south of his father's home. He had taken a district exam and was admitted to a mission school that admitted only a small number of the brightest Africans. The teachers of the school, impressed by his intelligence, overlooked some of his pranks. However, it was his rebelliousness in the end that caused him to be expelled. He returned home, and when his father found out, he was furious. He told Barack Sr. that if he didn't behave properly, he would have no use for him. His father arranged for him to travel to Mombassa to take a job as a clerk for an Arab merchant, telling his son that now he would see how much he could enjoy himself, now that he had to earn money for his own keep. Having no choice but to obey his father, he took the job, but after an argument with the merchant, he quit. To find another job, he had to accept less pay, and his father told him he wouldn't amount to anything. Onyango told his son to leave because he had brought him shame.

Barack Sr. then went to Nairobi and found work as a clerk for the railroad. Influenced by Kenyan politics, he became bored with the job and began attending political meetings. After being arrested and put in jail for taking part in a meeting, he asked his father for bail, but his father refused. Upon his release, Barack Sr. was discouraged and began to think his father was right, perhaps he would amount to nothing. At 20 years old, he had no job, was estranged from his father, and was without money or prospects. And by now, he was married with a child, having met his first wife, Kezia, when he was 18. Attracted by her beauty, after a short courtship, he decided to marry her. Having no money for a dowry, he'd had to ask his father for help. When Onyango refused, Barack Sr.'s stepmother intervened, saying it would be improper for Barack to beg for help for a proper dowry. After a year of marriage, a son, Roy, was born. Two years later, a daughter, Auma, was born.

Barack Sr. took any work he could find to support his family. He was desperate and depressed because many of his classmates from the prestigious mission school were now leaving for university and some had gone to London to study. They all, he knew, could expect good jobs when they returned to a now liberated Kenya. Barack wondered if he would end up working as a clerk for the rest of his life. Then good fortune struck. Barack met two American women who were teaching in Nairobi. They loaned him books and invited him to their home. When they realized how intelligent he was, they suggested he continue his studies at university. Barack explained that he had neither a secondary school certificate nor sufficient funds to pay the tuition. The answer was to take a correspondence course to earn the needed certificate and pursue scholarship funds at a university in the United States. Once he began working on the lessons, he worked diligently, and a few months later, he sat for the exam at the American embassy. After several months, the acceptance letter came; he had earned the certificate. He still needed to gain acceptance to a university and find the funds to pay tuition and transportation expenses to the States. His father, once he saw how diligently Barack had worked, was proud and impressed; however, he wasn't able to raise the needed money. Determined to further his studies, Barack Sr. wrote letters to schools throughout the United States. The University of Hawaii responded, saying they would provide a scholarship for him to attend. Moving his pregnant wife and son to his father's compound, he left Nairobi in 1959; at the age of 23, he became the first African student at the University of Hawaii, where he studied econometrics. A short time later, in a Russian language class, he met a young American woman named Ann Dunham and fell in love. A short time later they were married and, in August 1961, Ann gave birth to a son. He was named after his father and grandfather, but was called Barry. In 1963, after graduating in three years and first in his class, Barack Sr. won another scholarship to pursue his Ph.D. at Harvard University. He accepted the scholarship, moved to Boston, and left his wife and son in Hawaii. His son, Barack, was two years old. Barack Sr. and Ann divorced. After leaving Harvard, Barack Sr. returned to Africa.

ANN DUNHAM, BARACK OBAMA'S MOTHER

Barack's grandparents eloped just before the start of World War II. His grandfather Stanley enlisted in the army, and he and his young wife, Madelyn, moved to an army base, where their daughter, Stanley Ann, was born. After the war, the family moved around, living in California, Kansas, and Texas, before relocating to Seattle. Stanley Ann was often teased because of her first name (so named because her father wanted a son), and Madelyn sometimes worried about her, especially when she tended to spend so much time alone. Barack writes in his book *Dreams from My Father* that his mother was something of a loner, being an only child who had moved around a lot during her youth, but that she was always cheerful and easy-tempered. He said she often had her head in a book and would sometimes wander off on a walk. When Madelyn came home from work, she often found Ann alone in the front yard, lying in the grass or on the swing, off in some world of her own.[15]

In his book, Barack also writes about racism and how his mother and grandparents were exposed to it while living in Texas. He tells the story of how Ann, at about 10 years old, made friends with a black girl. One afternoon, his grandmother came home from work and found Ann and her friend in the front yard, where they were being taunted by other children who stood in the street, yelling and throwing rocks. Realizing how scared the two girls were, she said, "If you two are going to play, then for goodness sake, go on inside." Madelyn reached for the black girl's hand, but the girl instead ran out of the yard and down the street. Upon hearing about the incident, Ann's father was angry, and the next day he visited Ann's school principal to complain about the other children's behavior. He also called the parents of the misbehaving children. The responses were all the same: white girls didn't play with "coloreds in this town." Whenever his grandfather spoke of racism to his grandson, he would add that he left Texas because of it. His grandmother felt a bit different, saying that racism wasn't even a part of their vocabulary at the time, adding that they both felt they should treat people decently and that was all there was to it.[16]

From Texas, the family moved to Seattle, where Ann graduated from high school. She dreamed of studying at the University of Chicago, but Ann's father said she was too young to live on her own, and so, in 1959, she moved to Hawaii with her parents and enrolled at the University of Hawaii. In one of her courses, Ann, a shy and awkward 18-year-old, met an African named Barack Obama. He was charming, with an acute intellect, and when he was introduced to her parents, they were wary at first but were soon won over. Barack and Ann were married in a civil ceremony. Their son, given the name of his father, was born on August 4, 1961. Ann and Barack Sr. later divorced. She then married Lolo Soetoro, an Indonesian student at the University of Hawaii. When Barack was six, he moved with his mother and Lolo to Indonesia. They lived in Jakarta, where Lolo worked as a geologist and Ann taught English to Indonesian businessmen at the American embassy as part of the U.S. foreign aid package to developing countries. Barack writes that his mother was grateful for Lolo's attentiveness toward his new stepson and that she guessed he wouldn't have treated his own son differently. He writes that his mother would picture herself at 24, moving with a child and married to a man whose history and country she knew little about, and that her very innocence was carried to another country right along with her passport.

She expected the new life to be difficult, so she learned all she could about Indonesia, then the fifth most populated country in the world, and its many tribes and dialects. Early on, she realized life was tougher than she thought it would be, in a country with endemic dysentery and fevers and cold-water baths and a hole in the ground instead of a toilet. What had drawn her to Lolo, after Barack Sr. had left her and Barack, was the promise of something new and important and the idea of helping him rebuild a country. She wasn't prepared, however, for the loneliness she encountered; her job at the embassy and the money she earned there helped, but they didn't help the loneliness she felt.[17]

Ann concentrated on Barack's education. There wasn't enough money to send him to the International School, where most of the foreign children were educated, so she arranged to supplement his Indonesian education with lessons from a correspondence course. Five days a week, beginning at four o'clock in the morning, she would make Barack his breakfast and give him English lessons for three hours before he left for school and she left for work. During these sessions, she also reminded Barack of his heritage. She described his grandparents' upbringing and his father's story, how he had grown up poor in a distant poverty-stricken country and how his life had been hard, how he had succeeded, and how he had lived his life according to his principles. She told him he should follow his father's example, that he had no choice because it was in his genes. She said, "You have me to thank for your eyebrows . . . but your brains, your character, you got from him." She brought home books on the civil rights movement, recordings of Mahalia Jackson, and the speeches of Martin Luther King. She told Barack stories of the schoolchildren in the South and how, even though they had to read the books discarded by the white children, they became successful doctors and lawyers. Barack learned from his mother that "To be black was to be the beneficiary of a great inheritance, a special destiny, glorious burdens that only we were strong enough to bear."[18]

The uneasy political situation in Indonesia and near constant loneliness and worry made Ann feel more and more apprehensive about life there. As she learned more about the Indonesian government and the difficult life for many of the Indonesian people, she took some comfort in the fact that, as a white American, she was protected and could leave if she wanted to. Ann also considered what the environment was doing to and for her son, being of mixed heritage, part white and part African. What resulted from all this uneasiness was a distance between Ann and her husband. Lolo had learned to live with those who ran the country and to work within its boundaries. He was able to obtain a new job with an

American oil company with the help of his well-connected brother-in-law. He moved his family to a better neighborhood, purchased a car and a television, and obtained a membership at a local country club. Although these luxuries made daily life easier, the additional demands of Lolo's new job caused more difficulties between Ann and Lolo. Despite the difficulties, Ann became pregnant and gave birth to a daughter, Maya. When Barack was 10, Ann sent him to Hawaii to live with her parents, deciding he needed to go to an American school. She stayed behind with Maya, promising her young son that she and his sister would soon follow. She separated from Lolo, and a short time later they were divorced. In the article "The Not-So-Simple Story of Barack Obama's Youth," which was published in the online edition of the *Chicago Tribune*, Barack's half sister Maya Soetoro-Ng said of Barack, their mother, and their grandparents, Stanley and Madelyn (Toots), "Looking back now, I'd say he really is kind of the perfect combination of all of them. All of them were imperfect but all of them loved him fiercely, and I believe he took the best qualities from each of them."[19]

There is no doubt that Barack's mother and his grandparents were important influences in his life. In his book *The Audacity of Hope*, Barack writes extensively about family and specifically of his mother and grandmother. They were the ballast in his life, he writes, and it was the women who kept him and his family afloat and kept his world centered. He writes of his mother's love and clarity of spirit; it was because of her and his grandmother that he never wanted for anything important, and, from them, he understood the values that have always guided him.[20]

NOTES

1. Christine Brozyna, "Get to Know Barack Obama," ABC *News*, November 2, 2007.

2. Barack Obama, *Dreams from My Father* (New York: Three Rivers Press, 2004), 307.

3. Ibid., 369–372.

4. Ibid., 376–377.

5. Ibid., 394.

6. Ibid., 417.

7. Ibid., 407.

8. Ibid., 422.

9. Ibid., 13.

10. Ibid., 15.

11. Ibid., 16–17.

12. Kirsten Scharnberg and Kim Barker, "The Not-So-Simple Story of Barack Obama's Youth," *Chicago Tribune Online Edition*, March 25, 2007, http://www.chicagotribune.com/news/politics/chi-070325obama-youth-story.1.4006113.story.

13. Barack Obama, *Dreams from My Father* (New York: Three Rivers Press, 2004), 8.

14. Ibid., 417.

15. Ibid., 19.

16. Ibid., 20–21.

17. Ibid., 41–43.

18. Ibid., 50–51.

19. Kirsten Scharnberg and Kim Barker, "The Not-So-Simple Story of Barack Obama's Youth," *Chicago Tribune Online Edition*, March 25, 2007, http://www.chicagotribune.com/news/politics/chi-070325obama-youth-story.1.4006113.story.

20. Barack Obama, *The Audacity of Hope* (New York: Crown Publishers, 2006), 346.

Chapter 2

FORMATIVE YEARS IN HAWAII
AND INDONESIA

I was raised as an Indonesian child and a Hawaiian child and as a black child and as a white child. And so what I benefit from is a multiplicity of cultures that all fed me.

—*Barack Obama*

In 1959, just after her high school graduation, Ann Dunham moved with her parents to Honolulu, Hawaii. Her father, Stanley, had been offered a job at a new furniture store, and her mother, Madelyn, began working at a local bank. Ann, a shy, extremely bright 18-year-old, enrolled in the University of Hawaii. In one of her classes, Ann met a 23-year-old man named Barack Obama, the first African student accepted to the university. Studying econometrics, Barack was an intense scholar; he was also quite gregarious and had formed many friendships throughout the university community. Ann and Barack fell in love and were married, despite the misgivings of Barack's father, who wrote from Kenya that he didn't approve of the marriage. Barack's father threatened to have his son's visa revoked, which would have required his immediate return to Kenya. He didn't know the marriage had taken place until a few years later.

Ann's parents were wary at first but soon accepted their son-in-law. His charm, his intelligence, and the couple's obvious love impressed them. On August 4, 1961, Ann and Barack had a son they named Barack Hussein Obama—Barack after his father and Hussein after his grandfather. The son, born to a white American woman and a black African man, was called Barry. In 1963, Barack Sr. was awarded a scholarship to study at Harvard University for a Ph.D. Although the scholarship money was sufficient to support him, it was not enough to support Ann and their son. Barack Sr. went to Boston, leaving Ann and Barry, now two years old, in Hawaii. Ann and Barack Sr. divorced, and Ann continued her studies at the university. Ann's parents, Stanley and Madelyn (known as Toots, short for Tutu, the Hawaiian word for grandparents), were a constant presence in Barry's life.

Barry didn't know his father, except from the stories he heard from his mother and grandparents and from the photographs he found tucked away in closets. Barack writes in his memoir *Dreams from My Father* about an early memory of sitting on the floor with his mother staring at photos of his father's dark laughing face, his prominent forehead, and his thick eyeglasses. His mother told him about his father growing up in Kenya, as part of the Luo tribe, in a village named Alego. Barack listened as his mother told him about his father tending goats and attending a local school, where he was thought to have promise. She described how he had won a scholarship to study in Nairobi and was selected by Kenyan leaders and American sponsors to attend a university in the United States. She added that his father was expected to learn about Western technology and return to Africa with the skills to help create a new, modern Africa. She explained that his father had returned to fulfill that promise to his country. And even though she and Barry stayed behind, the bond of love survived the distance.[1] By the time Barry was old enough to listen to and remember the stories, his mother had begun a relationship with a man who would become her second husband.

After his father left to study at Harvard, Barry began to spend a good deal of time with his grandparents. He accompanied his grandfather to a park to play checkers and went fishing with him and his friends. All the while, he knew his father was missing. The stories he heard didn't tell him why his father had left or what life might have been like if he had stayed. Barack didn't blame his family for what was left out or what they didn't tell him. Instead, he created his own picture of his father. In his memoir, Barack wrote about finding an article that appeared in the *Honolulu Star-Bulletin* at the time of his father's graduation from the university. In the picture that accompanied the article, Barack describes his father as guarded and responsible, a model student, and an ambassador for Africa. Barack Sr., he writes, scoffed at the school's treatment of foreign students, who were forced to attend programs designed to promote cultural understanding, which he said was a distraction from the training the students were seeking. Barack writes that his father noted that other nations could learn from Hawaii how races are willing to work together toward a common development, adding that this was something whites in other places were unwilling to do. There is no mention in the article of Ann or their son, Barack notes; the omission of this information made him wonder whether this was on purpose, based on his father's pending departure from the family, or due to the fault of the reporter not asking more questions. Barack found the article about his father with his own birth certificate and vaccination records.[2] For years, Barack pictured his father in his mind, always wondering why he left. Years later, memories of his "ghost" of a father were triggered, sometimes by reading an article about Africa or seeing a group of children on a street corner. Barack might wonder if any of the children were without their fathers.

In December 2007, Barack said that thoughts of his father would "bubble up"; memories would come to him at random moments. "I think about him often. . . . Men often long for their fathers' approval, to shine in their fathers' light." And when asked how he feels about his father today, what is the dominant emotion in these thoughts, Barack answers, "I didn't know him well enough to be angry at him as a father. Mostly I feel a certain sadness for him, and the way that his life ended up unfulfilled, despite his enormous talents."[3]

LIVING IN INDONESIA AND A NEW FATHER

I have wonderful memories of the place [Indonesia], but there's no doubt that, at some level, I understood that I was different. It meant that I was, maybe, not part of the community as much as I might have been, otherwise. On the other hand, it also gave me an appreciation of what it means to be an American.[4]

Barack was two when his father left for Boston and Harvard Law School. When he was four, his mother met an Indonesian man named Lolo Soetoro, also a student at the University of Hawaii. They dated for two years and were married. During the two-year courtship, Lolo spent a great deal of time at the Dunham household, and, by the time Ann told Barry that she and Lolo were to be married and would be moving to a faraway place, Barry, now six, wasn't surprised and didn't object. Lolo returned to Indonesia, and Ann remained in Hawaii to make necessary preparations to move. Arriving in Jakarta, Ann and Barry were met at the airport by Lolo and groups of soldiers wearing brown uniforms and carrying guns. In anticipation of their arrival, a new home had been built, and Barry was already enrolled in a school. As they rode to their new home in a borrowed car, Barry gazed at the landscape of the new place—the villages, forests, rice paddies, water buffalo, congested streets and markets, and men pulling carts loaded with goods.

The new house, located on the outskirts of town, was made of stucco and red tile and had a mango tree in the courtyard. When he arrived at the new home, Barry's stepfather presented him with a gift: an ape named Tata, brought from New Guinea. Another surprise were the animals in the backyard, including chickens, ducks, a yellow dog, two birds of paradise, a cockatoo, and two baby crocodiles in a pond at the back of the property. Dinner on their first night in their new home included a hen that a friend of Lolo's killed while Barry watched. Later, lying beneath a mosquito net canopy, Barry tried to sleep as he listened to chirping crickets. He could barely believe his good fortune.

Barack writes in his memoir that, after being with Lolo for two years, his face had become familiar. In less than two years, Barack had learned the language, customs, and legends of Indonesia. He survived chicken pox, the measles, and the scratches suffered from his schoolteachers' bamboo switches. His best friends were the children of the farmers and the servants, and together they ran the streets, looking for odd jobs and flying kites. Lolo had taught him to eat raw green peppers, dog meat, snake meat, and grasshoppers. He wrote to his grandparents and gladly accepted the boxes of chocolate and peanut butter they sent. In his letters, Barack didn't mention some aspects of his life—those that he found too difficult to explain—like the faces of the farmers when the rains didn't come or when the rains lasted for over a month and the farmers had to rescue their goats and hens as their huts were washed away. He didn't describe the frequently violent world that he was quickly learning about, the world that was sometimes cruel and often unpredictable.

At the end of the day, when she returned from her work at the American Embassy, he talked with his mother about what he had seen, and she would stroke his forehead and try to explain to him as best as she could. He turned to Lolo for guidance and instruction, finding him easy to be with, glad that Lolo introduced him as his son to his family and friends. When Lolo explained the scars on his legs that came from the leeches that stuck to him and his fellow soldiers as they marched through the swamps in New Guinea, he told Barry that it hurt when the skin was singed after using a hot knife to remove the leeches. He said, "Sometimes you can't worry about hurt. Sometimes you worry only about getting where you have to go." He told Barry that he killed a man because the man was weak. He said, "Men take advantage of weakness in other men . . . better to be strong . . . if you can't be strong, be clever and make peace with someone who's strong . . . but always better to be strong yourself. Always."[5]

Before Ann and Barry moved to Indonesia, she tried to learn all she could about life there. She was prepared for most of what she encountered, but she didn't expect the loneliness. Lolo had changed since he left Hawaii. When he left Hawaii to prepare a home for his bride and her son, they were apart for a year. During that time, he lost the energy he had as a student in Hawaii, and his dream of teaching at a university upon his return to Indonesia also vanished. Ann later found out that Lolo and all the Indonesian students studying abroad were ordered to return home by the Indonesian government. When he landed in Jakarta, Lolo was questioned by army officials and was conscripted to serve in the army in the jungles of New Guinea for a year. The vitality that had attracted Ann to Lolo while they were students at the university was gone, and, as a result, Ann was lonely; her life wasn't what she'd hoped it would be.

Her job at the American Embassy helped her cope, as did the money she earned there and the friendships she made. At the embassy, Ann learned what was going on in the government—news and information she couldn't get otherwise. Knowing she could leave if she wanted or needed to, and knowing her white race and American passport protected her, she felt some comfort. What worried her more was what the situation was doing or might do to her son. Lolo, who had been working as a geologist, obtained a job in a government relations office of an American oil company with the help of his well-connected brother-in-law. A higher income enabled the family to move to another neighborhood, purchase a car and a television, and obtain a membership in a country club. All this did little to help Ann understand and cope. She decided she needed to concentrate on Barry's education, outside of what he learned at the Indonesian school. There was no money to send Barry to the International School that most of the foreign children attended, so she supplemented his education with lessons from a U.S. correspondence course. Five days a week, at four o'clock in the morning, while Barry ate his breakfast, she gave him English lessons before he left for school and she left for work. As well, she would remind Barry of his heritage, describing how his father grew up poor in a poverty-stricken country, telling Barry that hard work and living life according to strict principles was how his father lived, and Barry had no choice but to do the same. Besides the correspondence course, she brought home books on the civil rights movement, music recordings of black singers, and copies of speeches by Rev. Martin Luther King Jr.; she told him stories about the black children in southern U.S. states who were forced to read books discarded by the white children. They succeeded despite their hardships, she said. She told Barry that to be black was to be the beneficiary of a great inheritance and a special destiny.[6]

Ann spent many hours supplementing what Barry was learning in the Indonesian school. She was adamant that he learn about race, heritage, and about being an American. All of the information confused Barry about who he was, where he came from, and his mixed-race heritage.

When he looked in the mirror, he wondered if something was wrong with his reflected face. Watching television shows with black actors and thumbing through the Sears, Roebuck Christmas catalog his grandparents sent to him only confused him further. Most of what he felt and observed he kept to himself, believing that either his mother didn't see or feel the same way or she was attempting to protect him. Through it all, he trusted his mother's love for him, despite feeling that what she had taught him was incomplete somehow. Barack lived in Indonesia for four years. During that time, Ann gave birth to a daughter named Maya. When Barack was 10, Ann sent him back to Hawaii to live with her parents, believing he needed to attend school there rather than continue his education in Indonesia. She promised her young son that she and Maya would soon join him in Hawaii.

Barack's time in Indonesia stayed with him long into adulthood. In his book *The Audacity of Hope*, published in 2006, he writes that he is haunted by memories of his life in Bali. He thinks about how packed mud felt beneath his bare feet as he walked through rice paddies, of how the sky at sunrise looked behind volcanic peaks, fruit stands along the road, and the muezzin's call at night. He writes that he hopes to take his wife, Michelle, and their two daughters there someday, so he can share something of his life as a child with them. But his plans, he says, are always delayed, and he worries that what he might find there now wouldn't match his memories. He adds that, even with today's cell phones, direct flights, and 24-hour news coverage and Internet cafes, Indonesia feels more distant to him than it did 30 years ago. He fears, he says, that the land where he spent four years of his childhood has become a land of strangers.[7]

MOVING BACK TO HAWAII AND LIVING WITH GRANDPARENTS

Traveling by himself and confident that his grandparents would be at the airport to meet him, Barry arrived in Honolulu carrying a wooden mask that the Indonesian copilot, a friend of his mother's, had given him. Sure enough, his grandparents Stanley and Toots were there, waving and anxious, welcoming their grandson home again. Toots put a garland of gum and candy around his neck, and Stanley, whom Barry called Gramps, put his arm around Barry's slim shoulders. On the way to his grandparents' apartment, Gramps and Toots talked about what they were having for dinner that evening and how Barry would need new clothes for school. Barry was 6 when he left Hawaii, and now he was 10. For four years, he'd lived in a completely different place, and the change was dramatic. Suddenly he felt as if he would be living with strangers. While he had been away, his grandparents had sold their house and had moved into a two-bedroom apartment. His grandfather had left the furniture business and was selling insurance. He had landed in something familiar, but very different.

As he listened to his grandparents, Barry remembered how his mother had said it was time for him to attend an American school, since he had completed all the lessons from the correspondence course. She said she and Maya would join him soon, in a year at most, and that she'd try to be there for Christmas. She had reminded him of previous summers, filled with ice cream and days at the beach, and told him that he wouldn't have to wake up at four o'clock in the morning to do his lessons. Over the course of the summer, Barry adapted to life with his grandparents. Every morning, Toots left the apartment in her tailored suit and high-heeled shoes to go to her job at the bank, and Gramps would make phone calls, trying to sell insurance policies. As the summer came to a close, Barry became anxious about starting school. The previous summer, while visiting his grandparents, he had interviewed for admission to the prestigious Punahou Academy, a prep school started by missionaries in 1841. After one of the interviews, Barry and Gramps were given a tour of the school grounds by the admissions officer, a woman who had grilled Barry on his academic and career goals. The school's green fields and shade trees spread over several acres and included tennis courts, swimming pools, and, in the glass-and-steel buildings, photography studios. On the tour, Gramps was so impressed that he told Barry, "Hell, Bar, this isn't a school. This is heaven. You might just get me to go back to school with you."[8] Barry's acceptance at the school was a contributing factor in his mother's decision to send him back to Hawaii. The waiting list was long, the admission standards strict, and Barry's admission was helped along by his grandfather's boss, a graduate of the school.

On Barry's first day of the fifth grade, Gramps took him to school and insisted that they arrive early. As the teacher took attendance, she read Barry's name. There were giggles throughout the classroom. The teacher, who had called him by his African name, Barack, told him that Barack was a beautiful name and that she had lived in Kenya. She asked what tribe Barry's father was from, and when he answered the Luo tribe, the children laughed. Throughout the day, Barry was in a daze, especially after one of his classmates asked to touch his hair and another asked if his father ate humans. When he returned home after school and was asked about his day, he went into his room and closed the door. As one of the few black students at the elite school, Barry stood out among the children of Hawaii's wealthy, most of whom were white and Asian. As Rik Smith, a black student two years older than Barack, described it for the *Chicago Tribune* in March 2007, "Punahou was an amazing school. But it could be a lonely place. Those of us who were black did feel isolated—there's no question about that."[9]

Barry's novelty gradually wore off, yet his sense that he didn't belong at the prestigious school lingered. His clothes were different, and the same shoes he wore in Jakarta were neither suitable nor the least bit fashionable. Many of his classmates had been together since kindergarten and lived in the same neighborhoods. For Barry, at 10 years of age, life seemed difficult. Slowly, he made a few friends, but his life, for the most part, consisted of walking home from school, watching television while Gramps took his afternoon nap, completing his homework before dinner, and falling asleep listening to music on the radio. One day, a telegram arrived, announcing Barack Sr. was coming for a visit.

At school, Barry told his classmates that his father was a prince and that his grandfather was a chief of the tribe. He told them that his last name, Obama, meant "burning spear."[10] Because the story brought acceptance with his classmates, Barry began to believe the story he told; yet he knew he was telling a lie. His mother, who was visiting for Christmas as promised, seemed apprehensive of the pending visit and tried to reassure her son. She told him she had maintained a correspondence with his father and that he knew all about Barry's life in Indonesia and in Hawaii. She told Barry his father had remarried and that Barry now had five brothers and a sister living in Kenya. She said his father had been in a car accident and that his visit was part of his recuperation after a long hospital stay. Ann said Barry and his father would become good friends, and she spent hours giving Barry information about Kenya. After listening to his mother talk about Kenya and his father's life there, Barry visited the public library and read a book on East Africa. He read about his father's tribe and how they raised cattle, lived in mud huts, and ate cornmeal and yams. He left the book open on the library table. On the day his father was to arrive, Barry left school early. Filled with apprehension, he stood at the door of his grandparents' apartment and rang the doorbell. When his grandmother opened the door, there stood his father, a tall, dark figure who walked with a limp. His father crouched down and put his arms around Barry. He said, "Well, Barry, it is a good thing to see you after so long. Very good." He led him by the hand into the living room and said he'd heard Barry was doing well in school. When Barry didn't answer, his father said he had no reason to be shy about doing well in school and that his brothers and his sister were also excelling in their schoolwork. He told Barry this was in his blood. He gave Barry three wooden figurines: a lion, an elephant, and an ebony man in tribal dress beating a drum. When Barry mumbled a thank you, his father looked at the carvings, touched his son's shoulder, and said, "They are only small things."[11] In his memoir, Barack writes that, after a week of seeing his father, he decided that he preferred the more distant image of his father—one that he could change or even ignore. His father, he wrote, remained something unknown, something volatile and somewhat threatening.[12]

Barack Sr. spent a month in Hawaii, recuperating from his injuries suffered in the car crash and reconnecting with his son. Looking back on it, Barack writes in his memoir that he was often silent around his father, and he was fascinated by the power his father seemed to have over his mother and grandparents at first. Barack remembers his father's laugh, his deep voice, and how he stroked his beard. Barry's grandmother was more vocal about her opinions, and his grandfather seemed more energetic around his father. For the first time, Barry thought of a father as something real, and maybe even a permanent presence in his life. Then, after a while, tensions rose. His mother looked strained, and his grandmother would mutter to herself; his grandfather complained about this or that, until one evening talking turned to shouting over whether Barry should watch a holiday television show. Barack Sr. thought his son watched too much television and that he should work harder on his studies. Their voices grew louder, and Barry stayed in his room. After the argument was over, 10-year-old Barry began to count the days until his father would leave, hoping life would return to normal.

Before his father returned to Kenya, he was invited to speak at Barry's school. Barack Sr. spoke to Barry's class about boys proving their manhood, the elders of the tribe, and about his country's struggle to be free from British rule. The class applauded his father and a few asked questions; one of the teachers said he had an impressive father, and a classmate thought his father was very "cool." Two weeks after visiting Barry's school, Barack Sr. returned to Kenya, leaving Barry with real images and genuine memories of his absent father.

Barack continued his education at the Punahou Academy. By the time he was in his teens, there were still only a few black students at the school. Since Barack Sr. had visited, life had been relatively calm, but, as Barry got older, life became more complicated. There were calls from the principal's office, a part-time job, marginal report cards, and a few awkward dates. There was also the usual comparison with friends and what they had and what Barry did not have. By this time, Ann and Lolo had separated and she and Maya returned to Hawaii to pursue her master's studies in anthropology. For three years, the three of them lived in a small apartment near the academy, supported by the grants Ann had received. She often reminded Barry that she was a single mother going to school and raising two kids, and the less than perfect housekeeping and the lack of food in the refrigerator were all a part of their life. Despite his claims of independence, and sometimes age-driven sullen attitudes, he did his best to help his mother with shopping, laundry, and looking after his sister. When the time came for Ann to return to Indonesia to complete her fieldwork in anthropology, she wanted Barry to return with her and Maya. His response was an immediate no, knowing he could live with his grandparents again. According to his sister Maya, "I don't imagine the decision to let him stay behind was an easy one for anyone. But he wanted to remain at Punahou. He had friends there, he was comfortable there, and to a kid his age, that's all that mattered."[13] The arrangement to live with Gramps and Toots, who were very much like parents to Barry, was what he wanted. He realized he was growing up to be a black man in America; the trouble was, neither he nor anyone around him knew what this meant. His father had given him few clues in the sporadic letters he sent. The letters were about his family in Kenya and Barry's progress in school and noted that he and his mother and sister were welcome at any time in Kenya. Neither Gramps nor his few black friends offered much advice.

One outlet for Barry was basketball. By the time he was in high school, Barry was on the varsity squad, but not a starter. Known as "Barry O'Bomber" because of his long jump-shot ability, it was on the court where Barry met other blacks whose confusion and anger would help shape his own. According to Alan Lum, who later coached at Punahou and also taught elementary school there, Barack was always the first to confront coaches when he felt they weren't fairly allotting playing time, and he wasn't shy about advocating for himself or his fellow players. He added, "He'd go right up to the coach during a game and say, 'Coach, we're killing this team. Our second string should be playing more.'"[14] Barry also went to the gym at the university, where black men played. There he learned about an attitude that came from what one did, not from someone's father or family. On the court, Barry found a community where being black wasn't a disadvantage.

By the time he was in high school, Barry was feeling what it meant to be black in Hawaii, and he was searching for his own identity. He writes in his memoir about giving a classmate a bloody nose when the boy called him a coon and about an elderly neighbor who felt scared when he got on the apartment building elevator and told the building manager that Barry had been following her. He writes about a tennis pro who told him not to touch the schedule on the board because his color might rub off and then asked Barry if he could take a joke. He remembers his white assistant basketball coach whispering within earshot that his team shouldn't have lost to a "bunch of niggers." When Barry told him to shut up, the coach calmly explained that it was an obvious fact that "there are black people, and there are niggers . . . those guys were niggers."[15] Barry was learning about the term *white folks*, and it was uncomfortable for him. He was aware of the low expectations some white people had for him. He knew that people were satisfied as long as he was courteous and smiled and made no sudden moves. He wrote in his memoir, "Such a pleasant surprise to find a well-mannered young black man who didn't seem angry."[16] When he would speak with his friend Ray, a black student two years his senior, he would refer to white folks, and then he would suddenly remember his mother, and his words would seem awkward or false. He would think of his grandparents and helping his grandfather dry the dishes after dinner and his grandmother saying she was going to bed, and the phrase *white folks* would flash in his mind. He had no idea, as a black man in a place far from the South, who he was. He just knew he was different. Moving back and forth between his black friends and his white family, living within the languages and cultures, he hoped the two worlds would somehow meet, despite always feeling that something wasn't right.

When Barack was a senior at Punahou Academy, he stopped writing to his father and his father stopped writing back. He had put his studies aside, still struggling with who he was, and experimented with drugs and alcohol to try to put the struggle out of his mind. Her fieldwork complete, his mother had returned from Indonesia, and she began to ask Barry questions about school, his friends, and where he was headed after high school. When he attempted to politely reassure her, she wasn't at all assured. She wondered whether he was being a bit casual about his future. His grades were slipping, and he hadn't started on college applications. Wasn't he concerned about the future? Answering that he thought he could stay in Hawaii and take some classes while working part-time, she responded that he could get into any school in the country with some effort. Barry graduated from Punahou and was accepted by several schools. He decided to attend Occidental College in Los Angeles, mainly because he had met a young woman vacationing with her family in Hawaii who lived in a suburb of Los Angeles. When asked by an old friend of his grandfather's, an elderly black poet named Frank who lived in a run-down part of Waikiki, what he expected to get out of college, Barack answered that he didn't know. Frank told Barack, "Well, that's the problem, isn't it? All you know is that college is the next thing you're supposed to do. And the people who are old enough to know better, who fought all those years for your right to go to college . . . the real price of admission." He added that Barack wasn't going to college to be educated, but to be trained—about equal opportunity and the American way—and to keep his eyes open.[17] In the fall of 1979, Barack left Hawaii for California, feeling like he was going through the motions of attending college and armed with an attitude he didn't know how to change.

NOTES

1. Barack Obama, *Dreams from My Father* (New York: Three Rivers Press, 2004), 9–10.

2. Ibid., 26–27.

3. Kevin Merida, "The Ghost of a Father," *Washington Post*, December 4, 2007, A12.

4. Christine Brozyna, "Get to Know Barack Obama," *ABC News*, November 1, 2007.

5. Barack Obama, *Dreams from My Father* (New York: Three Rivers Press, 2004), 36–41.

6. Ibid., 50–51.

7. Barack Obama, *The Audacity of Hope* (New York: Crown Publishers, 2006), 278–279.

8. Ibid., 58.

9. Kirsten Scharnberg and Kim Barker, "The Not-So-Simple Story of Barack Obama's Youth," *Chicago Tribune Online Edition*, March 25, 2007, http://www.chicagotribune.com/news/politics/chi-070325obama-youth-story.1.4006113.story.

10. Barack Obama, *Dreams from My Father* (New York: Three Rivers Press, 2004), 63.

11. Ibid., 65–66.

12. Ibid., 63.

13. Kirsten Scharnberg and Kim Barker, "The Not-So-Simple Story of Barack Obama's Youth," *Chicago Tribune Online Edition*, March 25, 2007, http://www.chicagotribune.com/news/politics/chi-070325obama-youth-story.1.4006113.story.

14. Ibid.

15. Barack Obama, *Dreams from My Father* (New York: Three Rivers Press, 2004), 80.

16. Amanda Ripley, David E. Thigpen, and Jeannie McCabe, "Obama's Ascent," *Time*, November 15, 2004, 74–81.

17. Barack Obama, *Dreams from My Father* (New York: Three Rivers Press, 2004), 97.

Chapter 3

COLLEGE AND COMMUNITY ACTIVISM IN CHICAGO

OCCIDENTAL COLLEGE

In the fall of 1979, as Barack left Hawaii to attend Occidental College in Los Angeles, Jimmy Carter was president, a first-class stamp cost 15 cents, and the average retail price of gasoline was 88 cents per gallon. In November, Iranian militants seized the U.S. Embassy in Teheran and held 63 Americans hostage for 444 days. For Barack, his new home didn't look, at least on the outside, much different from his home in Hawaii. It was sunny, there were palm trees, and the Pacific Ocean was nearby. On campus, the other students were friendly and the college instructors were encouraging; there were enough black students to form friendships—a sort of tribe where issues such as race and common concerns were discussed. However, he also found that many of his black friends in Los Angeles weren't necessarily concerned with the same complaints as his black friends in Hawaii. Most had the same concerns of white students: continuing with classes and finding a good job after graduation. Barack continued to search for an identity and struggle with his mixed race.

In his memoir, *Dreams from My Father*, Barack wrote that growing up in Hawaii instead of the more difficult streets and neighborhoods where many of his friends had lived might have left him without the same feeling of needing to "escape." For him, there was nothing he had to escape except his own inner doubts. He felt more like the black students who had grown up in the safer environment of the suburbs; their parents had already escaped from more difficult circumstances. They, he wrote, weren't defined by their color; they were individuals, refusing to be categorized.

One friend told Barack that she wasn't black, but multiracial, born of an Italian father and a mother who was part African, French, and Native American. She didn't feel she had to choose between them. She added that it wasn't white people who asked her to choose, but black people who were making everything racial and who were trying to make her choose.[1] Barack recognized himself in her and others who spoke the same way. And yet it caused him to question his race even more. As a result, he chose his friends carefully at Occidental, wanting some distance from those like his friend who pronounced herself a multiracial individual. He felt only white people were individuals and that others were confused. It was this confusion that made him keep questioning who he was, and he sought distance to prove to himself and others which side he lived on and where his loyalties were.

While at Occidental College, Barack went from being called Barry to being called Barack. This happened after he met a black student named Regina. He had seen her around campus, usually in the library or organizing black student events. At their first meeting, he was introduced by a mutual friend as Barack. "I thought your name was Barry," she said. "Barack's my given name. My father's name . . . it means 'blessed.' In Arabic. My grandfather was a Muslim." Regina repeated the name a few times and told him it was a beautiful name and asked why everyone called him Barry. He responded that it was habit, that his father had used it when he came to the States, and that it likely was easier to pronounce and helped his father fit in. In Regina's story, as she explained it the first time they met, he found a vision of the possibility of black life, a history that was fixed and definite. He envied her and her memories of a childhood in Chicago, with an absent father and a struggling mother, with her uncles, cousins, and grandparents laughing around a table. Her response to this was that she envied her new friend, wishing she had grown up in Hawaii like him. As a result of this friendship with Regina, Barack felt stronger and more honest with himself and that a bridge had developed between his past and his future.[2]

As a sophomore, Barack became involved with a divestment campaign at Occidental. As his role with the campus group expanded, he found his opinions were being heard, and, as a result, he searched for his own messages and ideas. When asked to give the opening remarks at a rally on campus, he explored his memories of his father's speech to his class at Punahou Academy and his father's power to transform words into real changes. At the rally, he was meek at first but then gained confidence as he looked out at the crowd. With a voice that at first was barely heard, he began to speak about the struggles, not between blacks and whites, not between the rich and the poor, but in fairness, dignity, and injustice and servitude; between commitment and indifference and between right and wrong. The crowd watched and listened and then began to applaud. He quickly realized a connection had been made. When it was time for him to leave the stage, he was reluctant to do so because he had more to say. However, later, when he was offered congratulations on his speech that others said was delivered from the heart, Barack had already decided it was his last speech. He felt he had no business speaking for black people, deciding instead he had nothing to say; the applause, he thought, only made *him* feel better, not those about whom he was asked to speak.

His friend Regina told him he was naive to believe he could run away from himself and avoid what he felt. She told him he needed to stop thinking that everything was about him. It wasn't about him, she told him; it was about people who needed his help, about children everywhere who were struggling, suffering, and who were not interested in his bruised ego. For Barack, this success on the stage and his feeling afterward of finding fault within himself were the result of fear—fear that he didn't belong, that unless he hid or pretended to be something he wasn't, he would remain an outsider, away from anyone who stood in judgment of him. He decided his identity might begin with his race, but it didn't end there. But still, he asked himself where did he belong? He was two years away from college graduation and had no idea of what he would do then. His childhood in Hawaii felt like a dream, and he knew he wouldn't return to settle there. And he felt that no matter what his father in Kenya might say, he couldn't claim Africa as his home. What he needed, he determined, was a community, a place where he could put down roots and test his commitments. He decided to take advantage of a transfer program between Occidental College and Columbia University in New York City.

COLUMBIA UNIVERSITY

In August 1981, when he was 20 years old, Barack arrived in New York to study political science and international relations at Columbia as a junior transfer student. After finding a place to live, he acclimated himself to the city, finding it a far different place from Los Angeles and certainly poles apart from Honolulu. New York City dazzled him; the beauty and the ugliness, the excess and the noise, the wealth and poverty all amazed him. In his memoir, *Dreams from My Father*, Barack writes of the city's allure and its power to corrupt. With the stock boom of the 1980s, he noticed that men and women barely out of their twenties were already enjoying great wealth. Uncertain of his ability for self-control and to lead a moderate lifestyle, and fearful of falling into old habits of drugs and alcohol, he saw temptation everywhere. What he saw happening was reminiscent of the poverty he saw in Indonesia and the violent mood of the young people in Los Angeles. Whether it was because of the high density of people in New York or the very scale of the city, he began to grasp the problems of race and class in the United States. He had hoped to find refuge in the black community in New York. But instead of finding a satisfactory life for himself—a vocation, family, and a home—he noticed that, for the most part, blacks working in the offices were the messengers and the clerks, not the occupants of the high-rise offices. Discussing what he found with friends and associates, he tried to determine his future in a place that seemed out of control, a place where obvious divisions were natural. With money, he found he could have a middle-class life and organize his life around friends, favorite places to hang out, and political affiliations. But he knew that if he stayed in Manhattan, living a middle-class life like his black friends, at some point his choices couldn't be changed. Unwilling to do this, he spent a year observing what the city had to offer, looking for a place he could enter and remain.[3]

Barack immersed himself in his studies, determined to buckle down and work hard. During his first summer in New York, Barack's mother and sister Maya came to visit him. While he worked full-time on a construction site during the day, they went sightseeing, and they would all meet for dinner and talk about what they had seen or done that day. Noticing an envelope he had addressed to his father, Barack's mother asked if they were arranging a visit and that it would be wonderful for them to get to know each other. She said she realized it might have been difficult for a 10-year-old to understand his father, but now that he was older, it was a good time for them to meet again. She hoped he didn't feel resentful, and she began to tell Barack that it wasn't his father's fault that he left, but that she had divorced him. She said her parents weren't happy about the marriage in the first place, but they had agreed, and that Barack's grandfather didn't approve of the marriage either. She said the three of them were to go to Kenya after Barack Sr. finished his studies. He chose to go to Harvard—despite receiving only enough money from the school for tuition and not enough to support a family—because he had to prove he was the best, and going to Harvard was the way to do it.

She told Barack that when his father came to Hawaii to visit, he wanted them to return to Kenya with him, but she was still married to Lolo, and it wasn't possible. Barack heard in his mother's stories about his distant, absent father and about the love between them, a black man and a white woman, and she was trying to help her son see his father in the same way. A few months later, Barack's father died. Instead of traveling to Africa for his father's funeral, he wrote to his father's family to express his condolences. He wrote in his memoir that he felt no pain at his father's passing, only a vague sense of a lost opportunity. Later, he wrote, he dreamed about his father and afterward dug out the letters he had received over the years. Remembering his father's visit so long ago, he realized how, even in his absence, his father's strong image gave him structure, something to live up to or to disappoint.[4]

Barack graduated from Columbia University in 1983. In his profile in a Columbia alumni magazine in 2005, Barack recalled his college years as "an intense period of study," saying, "I spent a lot of time in the library. I didn't socialize that much. I was like a monk."[5]

MOVING TO CHICAGO

In 1983, Barack decided to become a community activist, even though he didn't know anyone who made a living doing this job nor did he know what such a job's duties might be. When asked about it, he would answer that there was a need for a change in the mood of the country. Change, he decided, happened at the grassroots level, and he would organize black people to effect change. He was congratulated for his ideas, but most of his friends were skeptical. Barack was about to graduate from college, and, while his friends were mailing off their applications for graduate school, he was thinking of his mother, his father's death, about living in Indonesia, and Lolo; he thought about his friends at Occidental and at Columbia. All of these memories were a part of his story and his struggles and a part of the struggles of black people. He believed that through organizing, communities could be created and fought for, and through this, his own uniqueness could be defined.

To become an organizer, he wrote letters to every civil rights organization he could think of. He also wrote to elected black officials and to neighborhood councils and tenant rights groups. When he received no response, instead of being discouraged, he decided to find a job to pay off student debts and save some money. He was hired as a research assistant at a consulting firm. He was soon promoted to a financial writer, with an office and a secretary. Eventually, he had money in his bank account. One day, as he was writing an article on interest rates, his half sister Auma called. Barack and Auma had been writing over the years, and he knew she had left Kenya to study in Germany. The idea of her visiting the United States or of him visiting her in Germany had been discussed, but nothing came of it. For the first time, he heard his sister's voice as she asked if she could visit him. Just before she was scheduled to arrive in New York, she called to say one of their brothers had been killed in a motorcycle accident, and she was going to fly home to Kenya. After the call, Barack thought about his family in Africa, wondering just who they were and why he wasn't sad at the loss of his half brother. The timing of his first contact with his half sister Auma was a catalyst. The idea of being an organizer remained an idea that tugged at him. His personal wounds, his struggles to form an identity, and taking a path that he thought would relieve some of the pressures within him were all tied to being part of a community, a far more personal path than the one he was on as a financial writer. A few months after Auma's call, he resigned from the consulting firm and looked for a job as a community organizer. Once again, he wrote letters. After a month or so, he received a response from a prominent New York civil rights organization. The director reviewed his credentials and said he was impressed with his corporate experience and offered a position organizing conferences on drugs, unemployment, and housing. Barack declined the offer, wanting a job that was closer to what was happening on the streets and in the neighborhoods. Within six months, Barack was still unemployed and broke. He had nearly given up when he received a call from Marty Kaufman, who had started an organizing drive in Chicago and needed a trainee. When they met, Kaufman asked why a black man from Hawaii wanted to be an organizer. He asked if Barack was angry about something, noting that anger was a requirement and typically the only reason someone would be a community organizer. Marty was white, Jewish, in his late thirties, and from New York. He had started organizing during the 1960s and was now attempting to join urban blacks and sub-urban whites in the Chicago area to save manufacturing jobs. He needed someone to help him, and that someone had to be black. He told Barack that most of the work would be done through local churches. When he asked Barack what he knew about Chicago, one of Barack's answers was that he had followed the career of Harold Washington, just elected mayor, a black man not accepted by the white people of a segregated midwestern city. He said he had written to Mayor Washington for a job but hadn't received a response. Marty's job offer included a salary of $10,000 for the first year, and a $2,000 travel allowance to buy a car.[6] After giving the offer some thought, Barack packed his belongings and drove to Chicago.

For three years, Barack drove his battered Honda Civic to church and neighborhood meetings in an effort to effect changes. For him and the many other organizers working in Chicago, there were successes and failures, and, while progress was made in some areas, the goal of retaining industry jobs and creating new jobs wasn't accomplished. However, Barack kept at it with his positive outlook, determination, and drive to succeed. And what he did for three years on the South Side of Chicago affected him. He was 24 years old, doing what he felt he needed to do.

Barack had been to Chicago once before, just before his 11th birthday. The three-day visit was part of a summer trip touring the States with his grandmother, mother, and sister. When he returned to the city in his twenties to begin a new job, he remembered the visit, deciding this time the city seemed prettier to him. On his own for a few days, he drove around the city, visiting neighborhoods and landmarks, imagining other newcomers arriving there looking for work, or visiting the nightclubs to listen to legendary performers. Remembering the stories of people he had met in Hawaii, California, and New York, he looked for his own place and how he could take possession of the city.

As his new boss showed him around the South Side, Barack learned about the factories that had closed, industries that had left the area, and how, as a result, blacks, whites, and Hispanics had all lost jobs. They all had the same types of jobs at the factories and plants, and, despite living similar lives, they didn't have anything to do with one another when they left work. When Barack asked how and why they would work together now, he was told that they had to if they wanted to get their jobs back. The job losses and layoffs had swept the South Side, leaving unemployment, poverty, loss of pensions, and fears of losing homes. There was a common sense of betrayal throughout these communities. An organization of 20 churches formed the Calumet Community Religions Conference, or CCRC, and another eight churches joined an arm of the organization called the Developing Communities Project, or DCP.[7] And while the CCRC had been awarded a job placement program grant, Marty told Barack that things weren't moving along as quickly as anyone hoped and that to keep momentum, to get jobs back to that part of suburban Chicago, they needed to get the unions on board and keep everyone working together. It was Barack's job to get and keep everyone working together, to create some enthusiasm, and to provide steady progress so people in the affected communities would stay on board and jobs would return to the area.

Barack was handed a list of people to interview and was charged with the task of finding their self-interest. That was how people became involved in organizations, Marty said, because they believed they would get something out of the process. Once he found an issue, a self-interest, that people cared about, he could get them to take action, and with action, there would be power. Barack liked these concepts of issues, spurring action, power, and people's self-interest. For the first three weeks of his job, he worked around the clock. He soon realized that getting interviews was very hard work, and there was a lot of resistance to meeting. After a few interviews, he noticed common themes. Many people had grown up in different areas of the city but had moved to the South Side for work because homes there were more affordable, there were yards for their children, and the schools were better. People were searching for something better. When Barack turned in his first report of interviews, Marty told him, "It's still too abstract . . . if you want to organize people . . . go towards people's centers . . . what makes them tick . . . form the relationships you need to get them involved."[8] Barack wondered how he would ever steer what he was hearing into any action.

After being in Chicago about two months, with a few missteps and no success at organizing or effecting change, Barack scheduled a meeting at Altgeld Gardens, a public housing project of 2,000 apartments located on the edge of the South Side. The area was surrounded by a landfill, a sewage treatment plant, an expressway, and closed factories. It was a place to house poor black people. With an occupancy rate of about 90 percent, many of the apartments were well kept, yet everything about the housing seemed to be in a state of disrepair. Managed by the Chicago Housing Authority, there were rarely any maintenance workers on-site to fix the broken pipes, ceilings, and backed-up toilets. Contrary to the project's name, the children and others who lived there rarely saw anything that looked remotely like a garden.

Barack scheduled a meeting at a Catholic church at Altgeld to meet with leaders of the community to discuss the organizing efforts. He knew from his meetings with Marty and the local unions, and with organizers who lived in the communities he was trying to change, about unemployment, lack of job training, how desperate it was in the communities, and why morale was so low among organizers. When he walked into the meeting, the leaders told him they were quitting. They assured him it wasn't because of him or his work; it was because they were tired and frustrated, and they didn't want to make promises to their neighbors and then have nothing happen. For Barack, at first there was panic, then anger. He was angry that he had come to Chicago in the first place, and he was angry with the leaders for being shortsighted. He told the small group of community organizers that he didn't come to Chicago because he needed a job, but because he heard there were people there who were serious about doing something to change their neighborhoods. He said he was there and was committed to helping them, and if they didn't believe anything had changed after working with him, then they should quit. Surprised at what he said, the group discussed what had and hadn't happened in the past and agreed they would give it a few more months. Barack agreed to concentrate on Altgeld Gardens and the problems facing the community.

After discussing the meeting with Marty, Barack stepped up his efforts to find more leaders in the neighborhood. One of the ideas was to hold a series of street-corner meetings. At first, Barack was skeptical that any of the area residents would come to meetings held out in the open on street corners. Slowly, however, people came. When they were told that the local church at Altgeld was part of a larger organizing effort and that the leaders wanted them and their neighbors to talk about what they always complained about while sitting at their kitchen tables, they answered that it was about time their complaints were heard. After a few corner meetings, the group numbered close to 30 people from the neighborhood. Slowly, there was some movement toward community organizing.

As Barack concentrated his efforts on Altgeld Gardens, he scheduled meetings to find solutions for the unemployment throughout the community. One such meeting was with an administrator of a branch of the Mayor's Office of Employment and Training (MET), which helped to refer people to training programs. Unfortunately, the local office was a 45-minute drive from Altgeld Gardens, hardly convenient for the neighborhood or the people who lived there. By the time Barack and the three community leaders arrived for their appointment, the administrator had left the office. They were given brochures with a list of the programs offered by the office throughout the city; none were located anywhere near Altgeld Gardens. Barack decided this was the issue he and his community leaders would concentrate on. They would push for a training center for the South Side and drafted a letter to MET. A director of MET agreed to meet with the organizers at the Gardens. At the meeting of close to 100 people, the administrator promised to have an intake center in the area within six months. Feeling elated at his first success, Barack decided he could do the job of community organizing.[9]

As Barack continued his interviews, Marty encouraged him to take some time off and build a life away from his job. Personal support was important, he said; without it, an organizer could lose perspective and burn out. When he wasn't working, Barack was mostly alone. Barack had developed friendships with some of the leaders of the organization, seeing them both professionally and socially. He writes in his memoir, Dreams from My Father, that the leadership was teaching him that the self-interest he was looking for extended beyond the issues and that beneath people's opinions were explanations of themselves. Their stories of terror and wonder, with the events that haunted and inspired them, made them who they were. This realization, he writes, was what allowed him to share more of himself with the people he was working with, to break out of the isolation that he carried with him to Chicago. He was afraid, at first, that his prior life would be too foreign for their feelings and opinions. Instead, when the people he worked with listened to his stories of his grandparents, mother, father, and stepfather, of going to school in Hawaii and Indonesia, they would nod their heads or shrug or laugh. They wondered how someone with his background had ended up so countrified and were puzzled by him. Why would he want to be in Chicago when he could be back in Hawaii? Their stories, in response to his stories, helped him bind the two worlds together, and they gave him a sense of place and purpose that he'd been looking for. He found that Marty was right—there was always a community there if you dug deep enough.[10]

Meanwhile, after writing to each other and speaking on the phone for years but never having met, Barack's half sister Auma came to Chicago for a visit. Immediately, there was a connection; their conversation was natural and easy, and the love they shared was fierce. He told her about New York, his work as an organizer in Chicago, his mother and Maya, and his grandparents. She'd heard about all of them from their father and felt like she already knew them. Auma told Barack about studying in Germany and about finishing her Master's degree in linguistics. As they talked, she referred to their father as the Old Man. The description felt correct to Barack: familiar, distant, and someone not understood. Barack took Auma on a tour of Chicago and introduced her to three members of the leadership. It was evident to Auma that her half brother was well respected and liked. She asked Barack if he was doing his work for them, the communities, or for himself.

As they spent time together, Auma told Barack stories of their father. She said she really didn't know him and that maybe no one did. She told him about Roy, her brother (Barack's half brother); Ruth, Barack Sr.'s white American wife; and Ruth and Barack's two sons. Barack heard about how their father had made a trip to Germany to see Auma; it was a time when he began to explain himself to her. She told Barack that their father always talked about his namesake and how he would show Barack's picture to everyone, telling them how well he was doing in school, that the letters Barack's mother sent to Kenya comforted their father, and how he would read them aloud over and over again, shaking the letter in his hand and saying how kind Ann had been to him. When the stories ended, Barack felt dizzy with the all the new information about his father and his extended family in Africa. All his life he'd carried an image of his father—an image he had rebelled against and never questioned, and one he had later tried to take for his own. He writes in his memoir that his father had been a brilliant scholar, a generous friend, and a leader, and, through his absence, he had never foiled this image. He hadn't seen his father shrunken or sick, his hopes ended or changed, his face full of regret or grief. It was his father's image, a black man from Africa, that he sought for himself, and his father's voice had remained "untainted, inspiring, rebuking, granting or withholding approval," and he could hear him say his son wasn't working hard enough and that he needed to help his people's struggle. The image he had always had changed after hearing Auma's stories. The curtain had been torn away, and he could now do whatever he wanted to do; his father no longer had the power to tell him otherwise. His father was no longer a fantasy and could no longer tell him how to live.[11] After a 10-day visit, as she prepared to board her plane back to Germany, Auma told Barack that they both needed to go home, to see their father there. The idea gave Barack much to think about.

As the organization's influence and successes grew, so did Barack's reputation. He began to receive invitations to serve on boards and to conduct workshops, and he became familiar with local politicians. The leadership of the community organization—those with whom he had worked so closely and those with whom he shared the successes in the neighborhoods—saw him as someone who could do no wrong. He had found a home within a community. He developed his listening skills and learned about strategies and bringing varied people together. He discovered the importance of personal stories in politics and a faith in ordinary citizens that continued to influence his work in politics in later years. He continued his work as an organizer, taking on asbestos contamination and cleanup at Altgeld Gardens, education and the state of the public schools on the South Side, and youth counseling and a network that would provide at-risk teenagers with mentoring and tutoring and involve parents in the planning process for reform. There were more successes and disappointments, but he kept going.

Of his time as a community organizer in Chicago, Michael Evans, of the Developing Communities Project (DCP), remembers Barack saying, "'You can only go so far in organizing. You help people get some solutions, but it's never as big as wiping away problems.' It wasn't end-all. He wanted to be part of the end-all, to get things done." Another member of the DCP, Loretta Augustine-Herron, said of Barack that he was "someone who always followed the high road," and she remembered him saying, "You've got to do it right . . . be open with the issues . . . include the community instead of going behind the community's back . . . you've got to bring people together. If you exclude people, you're only weakening yourself. If you meet behind doors and make decisions for them, they'll never take ownership of the issue."[12]

Barack maintained his ties to the DCP long after he had left the organization. At a DCP convention in 2004, he told the members, "I can't say we didn't make mistakes, that I knew what I was doing. Sometimes I called a meeting, and nobody showed up. Sometimes preachers said, 'Why should I listen to you?' Sometimes we tried to hold politicians accountable, and they didn't show up. I couldn't tell whether I got more out of it than this neighborhood. I grew up to be a man, right here, in this area. It's a consequence of working with this organization and this community that I found my calling. There was something more than making money and getting a fancy degree. The measure of my life would be public service."[13]

After three years of community organizing in Chicago, Barack grew restless, and, in 1988, he decided to leave Chicago for Harvard Law School. Before he moved to Boston, Barack went to Kenya to see Auma, who had moved back there after finishing her studies in Germany, and to meet and get to know his father's family. It was an important trip for this young man who continued to struggle with his identity, who needed to make sense of who he was, where he had come from, and where he wanted to go in the future. His father's image still haunted him, and he hungered for a clearer picture.

NOTES

1. Barack Obama, *Dreams from My Father* (New York: Three Rivers Press, 2004), 98–100.

2. Ibid., 104–105.

3. Ibid., 120–122.

4. Ibid., 127–129.

5. Janny Scott, "Memories of Obama in New York Differ," *New York Times*, October 29, 2007.

6. Barack Obama, *Dreams from My Father* (New York: Three Rivers Press, 2004), 142.

7. Ibid., 150.

8. Ibid., 158.

9. Ibid., 164–186.

10. Ibid., 187–190.

11. Ibid., 218–221.

12. David Moberg, "Obama's Community Roots," *The Nation*, April 3, 2007.

13. Ibid.

Chapter 4

A TRIP TO KENYA AND HARVARD LAW SCHOOL

LEAVING THE DEVELOPING COMMUNITIES PROJECT, ACTIVISM, AND THE SOUTH SIDE OF CHICAGO

Barack received his acceptance to Harvard Law School in February 1988. He announced to his coworkers, volunteers, and church ministers that he would be leaving in May and moving to Boston in the fall. Months before, he had told Johnnie, the man he'd hired away from a downtown Chicago civic group, of his decision. Johnnie, Barack knew, would carry on the work of the organization. Hiring him had lightened Barack's workload and had allowed him to believe that their hard work was making real differences for the people living on Chicago's South Side. Johnnie's response to Barack's leaving was more than positive. He told Barack that he knew it was just a matter of time before he left the Developing Communities Project, and he knew Barack had many options. He said that the choice between Harvard and the South Side wasn't any choice at all, adding that he and the community leaders would be proud to see him succeed.[1] Barack appreciated Johnnie's support and confidence, and it made the decision to leave easier. Barack realized he needed a break from the work of community activism, and he wanted to visit Kenya. His half sister Auma had returned to Nairobi from Germany and was teaching at a university. Having Auma in Kenya and having time before moving to Boston, it was the right time for an extended visit to his father's homeland.

The plan to attend law school came out of knowing how much he could learn. He wanted to gain knowledge of interest rates, corporate mergers, legislation, and how and why real estate ventures succeeded or failed. He also wanted to learn about influence and knowledge, vowing that, upon his return to Chicago, he would use what he learned effectively and powerfully to effect real changes in the Chicago neighborhoods he had come to know so well. Along with this vow to bring more to his activism, other thoughts were also on his mind. By going to Harvard, he was following his father's footsteps. Barack had dreams of effecting change in Chicago, and his father had dreams of using what he learned at Harvard to effect changes in Kenya.

From Johnnie and from the other leaders of the community organization where he had spent the last two-and-a-half years, Barack realized that no one begrudged his success, and they applauded him for what he wanted and felt he needed to do. He knew they didn't expect self-sacrifice, and they didn't judge; they knew that Barack's black heritage was enough of a reason for membership in their community. From these friends, supporters, and coworkers, he learned that his heritage was enough of a cross for him to bear. Barack had wanted to be part of a community, have a sense of belonging, and he had a desire for acceptance; this was, he realized, what drove him away from New York and to Chicago in the first place. Yet what he found in his work as a community activist was that, to be true to himself, he had to do what was right for others and have a commitment and faith. He also realized that to understand suffering required something else, too, but he had to find out what that something was. Faith in oneself wasn't enough.

After three years in Chicago, Barack made sure Johnnie and the other leaders of the organization knew what they needed to know and could carry on the necessary work he had started. Believing he was leaving the work in good hands, he left for Kenya.

KENYA, FAMILY, AND A FATHER'S LEGACY

Before going to Kenya, Barack planned a three-week trip to Europe, touring places he'd always heard about but had ever seen. However, instead of enjoying the trip, he felt edgy, nervous, and hesitant with strangers. By the end of the first week, he thought he'd made a mistake. Although Europe was beautiful, it wasn't a part of his own history, a part of who he was. He began to realize that the three-week trip was just delaying his journey to his father's home, a postponement of coming to terms with his father and his own past. He felt emptiness within, but would going to Kenya fill that space? His friends in Chicago assured him it would, that the trip was necessary, perhaps a pilgrimage of sorts, to find out about his father and his roots, a trip that might fill a gap that had always been there between him and his father.

Landing at Kenyatta International Airport, the homecoming he'd imagined quickly dissipated. No one was there to meet him. Abandonment and exhaustion quickly overwhelmed him. Searching for lost luggage, he was introduced to a young woman who recognized his family name, saying that Barack's father had been a close friend of her family. Barack realized this had never happened before. Never had anyone recognized the name Obama, nor had anyone ever remembered his father as Dr. Obama. For the first time, he felt comfort, an identity that name recognition provides. Suddenly, he realized that, in Kenya, no one would ask him to spell his name, nor would anyone mispronounce it. His name made him belong.

Not long after speaking with the African woman, Auma arrived. Trailing behind her was Barack's Auntie Zeituni, his father's sister. Kissing him on both cheeks, Auntie welcomed him home. On that first morning, as Barack rode in the car with Auntie Zeituni and his half sister, what he saw, smelled, and felt was strange but vaguely familiar. Then he realized that it all reminded him of his days in Indonesia with his mother and stepfather, Lolo. It was the same smell of burning wood and diesel fuel and the same expressions on people's faces as they made their way through the crowds going to work or to shop. Dropping off his Auntie at her job at a local brewery, she told Auma to take good care of Barry and to not let him get lost again. Barack asked Auma what she meant, and she told him that it was a local expression—when someone who hadn't been seen in a while returns, they are known as having been lost; she added that people who leave and never return, after promising to stay in touch, are thought to be "lost."

Barack spent his first day resting at Auma's apartment before absorbing Nairobi life by walking through the local marketplace. He saw Kenyans selling their wares, and he watched the tourists from Germany, Japan, the United Kingdom, and the United States shopping, eating, and setting themselves apart from the Kenyans selling their wares and serving them food. He remembered being a boy in Hawaii, making fun of the tourists with their pale white skin and skinny legs. He realized that the tourists in Kenya didn't seem funny; their self-confidence, their expression of freedom to roam with an obvious sense of superiority, felt somewhat insulting.

After spending the day walking through the Nairobi marketplace, Auma and Barack were invited to dinner at Aunt Jane's apartment. When he first met Jane, she reminded him that she was the one who had called him with the news that his father had died. At her home, a small crowd of family members had gathered to meet him. Besides his Aunt Jane, he met Auma's mother, Kezia. When she took his hand, she said in her native Swahili that her other son had finally come home. He shook hands with aunts, cousins, nephews, and nieces that evening, each greeting him cheerfully, each smiling as if meeting him was nothing new at all. After describing his work in Chicago, he told them he was going to study at Harvard in the fall. His Aunt Jane responded by saying it was good he was studying at the same place his father had studied. On the way back to her apartment, Auma told Barack about his Aunt Sarah, his father's older sister. She said he should visit with Aunt Sarah but that she wouldn't join him. When he asked why, Auma said there was a dispute over their father's estate, and Aunt Sarah was bitter over her brother's opportunities compared to the hard life she had experienced by being denied those same opportunities. She didn't believe the estate was worth much, but many, including Aunt Sarah, had expected much from Barack Sr. Auma said their father had made everyone believe he had so much when in reality he had little. And now that Barack had come to Kenya, he, too, was part of whatever inheritance there was, and he was one of the many family members competing for a portion of an estate that remained in dispute.

After only a few days in Nairobi, Barack could feel his father's presence in the streets where he walked, in the people passing by, in the laughter and the cigarette smoke. He thought the Old Man, as Auma called him, was there, asking his son Barack to see him and to understand. His family seemed to be everywhere, fussing over him as Barack Sr.'s lost son, wanting to provide for his needs, keeping him occupied, not wanting him to be alone. At first, he was grateful, noticing that this attention and closeness of family was different from the isolation found so often in the United States. But the closeness was tinged with tension, and it occurred to Barack that some of the tension came from the good fortune he had enjoyed in the United States, fortune that was in contrast with how his family and most Kenyans lived day by day. Conditions in Nairobi were difficult for everyone. From unemployment to few educational opportunities and living without a government safety net, there was truly only family to help in difficult circumstances. Now that Barack had an extended family, and with his good fortune, he had responsibilities. What they were, he did not yet know, because they were so different from the responsibilities he had back home.

As Barack struggled with his seemingly good life compared to a Kenyan's life and the resulting responsibilities to his Kenyan family, he was also learning more about his father and his father's role as head of the family. Zeituni told him that his father suffered because his heart was too big; he gave to anyone who asked him for something, and they all asked.

She told Barack that his father was under enormous pressure and that he shouldn't judge him too harshly; she cautioned Barack to learn from his father's life, saying that if he has something, everyone will want a portion of it. She said he must learn to draw a line somewhere and that if everyone is family, then no one is family. She said his father never understood this, and she cautioned Barack that he must.[2]

While in Kenya, Barack visited Ruth, one of his father's wives, and Mark, another half brother who was a student at Stanford University. While at Ruth's home, Barack looked at an album of photos of his father and Ruth and of Auma and her brother Roy. He saw pictures of his father and this part of his family on a beach vacation. They were seemingly happy scenes—scenes he had always dreamed about—of what his life would have been like had his father taken him and his mother back to Kenya. The photos were reflections of his own long-held fantasies that he had kept secret, of living under one roof with his father and mother and all his brothers and sisters. It was to him what might have been and how wrong it had turned out. The photos made him sad enough to look away. After leaving Ruth's, he and Auma talked about Mark and how difficult life was for him as a mixed-race child in Kenya. Barack then thought about his mother and his grandparents, and he realized once again how grateful he was for them—who they were and for the stories they told him. It was Zeituni's words—that if everyone is family, then no one is family—that kept him thinking. He had come to Kenya to make sense of many worlds that might be made into a harmonious whole. Instead, what was divided seemed to multiply. He was learning about his father, getting to know him long after he had died; he was meeting his extended family and learning what they meant to him and what he meant to them; he was learning about Kenya and about stereotypes; he was questioning his own spirit, ideas, courage, and ambitions. The longer he stayed, the more he knew; he also knew there were many more questions than there were answers.

As part of his Kenyan pilgrimage, Barack, Auma, Kezia, Auntie Zeituni, and his half brothers Roy and Bernard left Nairobi by train for the town of Kisumu and then on to the village of Alego, which, for Barack and his family, was "Home Squared," the ancestral home. In Alego was Granny, his grandfather's wife, who welcomed Barack with open arms, saying she had dreamed about the day she would meet him, the son of her son. She told Barack, in her native Luo language, that his arrival and his finally coming home had brought great happiness. Home Squared was a compound comprising a house with an iron roof and concrete walls, flowers, a large water tank, a few chickens, and a tall mango tree. Inside the small house was his father's Harvard diploma, photographs of Barack Sr. and an uncle who had moved to the United States and had never returned to Kenya, and photos of a young woman and two children standing behind an older man sitting in a high-backed chair. The picture was of Barack's grandfather, and the infant in the young woman's arms was Barack's father. After tea, Roy took Barack to two graves at the edge of the compound, near a cornfield. One was his grandfather's, whose headstone read *Hussein On-yango Obama, B. 1895, D. 1979;* the other grave was covered with tiles, with a bare space where a plaque should have been. After six years, Roy told Barack, there still was no plaque to say who was buried there.[3]

For Barack, the simple joy of being with Granny at the ancestral home was enhanced by everything he was doing and touching, the full weight of a circle that was beginning to close and that he might finally recognize himself as he was in that one place. When he found he couldn't communicate with Granny in the Luo language as he wanted to, and as she expected him to, he asked that Auma tell Granny that he wanted to learn Luo, but that it was hard to find time in the States, because he was very busy there. Granny said she understood but added that a man "can never be too busy to know his own people." At this point, he knew that this, too, was part of the circle, the fact that his life was not tidy or static, that after this important trip to Nairobi and to Home Squared there would always be hard choices to make.[4]

It was in the compound of his ancestral home in Alego, under a mango tree, that Barack asked Granny to tell him about his father's family. He asked her to start at the beginning. As Granny began to speak in Luo and Auma translated, Barack felt the wind lift and then settle, and he heard voices run together—three generations of voices running like a "current of a slow-moving stream . . . questions like rocks roiling with the water, the breaks in memory separating the currents, but always the voices returning to that single course . . . a single story."[5]

Before leaving Granny and Alego, Barack returned to the two graves at the edge of the compound. As he stood beside the grave without the plaque, Granny's stories came to life and he wept. When his tears were spent, calmness came over him and he felt the circle close. He realized who he was, what he cared about. He knew his life in the United States, the black life and the white life, the sense of abandonment he felt as a boy, and the frustrations and hopes he witnessed in Chicago were all connected to this place that was far away; it was a connection that was more than a name or the color of his skin. The pain he felt was the same pain his father felt, the questions were the same as his brothers' questions, and the struggle was his birthright.[6]

Barack returned to Nairobi with Auma. There were more family dinners, a few more arguments, and many more stories. He knew he would soon be returning to the United States and to another life altogether, and the trip became a true pilgrimage, a quest to find answers. And while some questions went answered, he knew that what he was looking for by going to Kenya he found in the stories he heard, the people he met, and what he saw and touched. The trip was like the baobab tree, he writes in his book *Dreams from My Father*, the tree that can go for years without flowering and can survive on practically no rainfall, the tree that some believe possesses a special power and that houses spirits and demons. It is because of their odd shape, he writes, their outline against the sky, that each can tell a story, having a character that is neither benevolent nor cruel, but enduring, and that the tree might walk away, except for its knowledge that "on this earth one place is not so different from another—the knowledge that one moment carries within it all that's gone on before."[7] Leaving his half sister Auma, and his father's family that was now his own family, in Nairobi, Barack returned to the States, ready to study law at Harvard.

HARVARD LAW SCHOOL

In the fall of 1988, Barack moved to Boston to attend Harvard Law School. He entered the prestigious school as an unknown man with an Afro hairstyle. His trip to Kenya had provided answers to many of his questions about his identity. Attending Harvard, just like his father, felt less complicated, and his reasons for attending seemed clearer. As a 27-year-old first-year law student, he was older than his classmates and, to some degree, more experienced. He had grown up in Hawaii and Indonesia, had toured Europe, and had visited family in Africa; he had also spent more than two years as a community activist in Chicago, giving him more experiences than many of his fellow classmates, most of whom entered law school right after college graduation. As a result, with the exception of playing pickup basketball games, Barack spent much of his time alone. After his first year, he spent the summer in Chicago as an intern at a law firm where he met his future wife, Michelle Robinson, also a Harvard Law graduate and a practicing attorney. When he returned to Harvard to continue his studies, Barack surprised his classmates by entering the race for president of the *Harvard Law Review*. This position, coveted by law school students, involved appointing editors, mediating disagreements, and accepting and rejecting articles submitted to the *Review*. The position could influence careers and was also considered a ticket to a high-powered legal position or an academic career. Barack was known to be one of the most driven students in his class. When his classmates first encouraged him to run for the presidency of the *Review*, Barack declined, stating he wanted to return to Chicago for the summer to continue his community organizing. A short time later, he agreed to add his name to the list of 19 candidates. Barack characterized his decision to compete for the position as almost impulsive: "It was probably one of those moments where I said, what the heck. I was an older student, 27. Most of my peers at the law review were a couple of years younger than I was. I thought I could apply some common sense and management skills to the job. I was already investing a lot of time in the law review, and my attitude was: Why not try to run the law review?"[8]

At the end of the day-long election process, Barack was one of two finalists for the job. In the end, the conservative faction, with its candidates already defeated, threw their support behind Barack. "Whatever his politics, we felt he would give us a fair shake," said Bradford Berenson, a former associate White House counsel in the George W. Bush administration.[9]

When Barack was announced as the winner of the most coveted position at one of the most prestigious institutions in the United States—the first black student to hold the spot in its 104-year history—he was inundated with interview requests from newspaper and magazine reporters. In the interviews, he was modest in his responses and careful with his answers. In one interview, he said, "The fact that I've been elected shows a lot of progress. It's encouraging. But it's important that stories like mine aren't used to say that everything is O.K. for blacks. You have to remember that for every one of me, there are hundreds or thousands of black students with at least equal talent who don't get a chance."[10] About his goals, Barack said, "I personally am interested in pushing a strong minority perspective. I'm fairly opinionated about this. But as president of the law review, I have a limited role as only first among equals." He said he would concentrate on making the review a forum for debate and would bring in new writers and push for livelier, more accessible writing.[11] Soon after his election to the *Law Review*, Barack was inundated with calls from publicists, publishers, and literary agents. Not long after beginning his post at the *Review*, Barack signed a contract with a publisher to write his memoir, *Dreams from My Father*.

For Barack, and likely any student who held the position as president of the *Harvard Law Review*, being elected was easier than serving. The climate at Harvard at the time was fractious, and there was a need for leadership. Barack found himself having to reject articles submitted by famous Harvard professors and having to get the editors to stop arguing and keep working. Bradford Berenson said, "I have worked in the

Supreme Court and the White House and I never saw politics as bitter as at *Harvard Law Review* in the early '90s. The law school was populated by a bunch of would-be Daniel Websters harnessed to extreme political ideologies."[12]

Barack, a now famous minority student, was part of a campus rife with racial politics. The *Law Review* was also struggling with the issue of whether affirmative action should be a factor in the selection of editors and whether voice should be given to those who argued that the legal system was biased against minorities. Barack had difficult choices to make. If he used his position to criticize Harvard, he would anger blacks and liberals. By speaking out, he risked putting himself and the *Law Review* in the center of debates. He found himself walking a delicate line. For the most part, each side listened to him, and both sides somehow felt Barack was endorsing their side. Both sides could often find justification in what Barack said. When he acknowledged that he had benefited from affirmative action, those who supported affirmative action were happy. Those who opposed affirmative action viewed his presidency as a triumph of meritocracy. In his speeches, he tried to steer clear of contention, stick to safe topics, and listen to others' opinions.[13]

Barack wrote in *Dreams from My Father* that, while he was in law school, he spent a lot of time in poorly lit libraries reading statutes and cases. He reflected that the study of law can be disappointing and a matter of applying narrow rules and difficult-to-understand procedures to reality. He observed that law is memory and a recording of long-running conversations and of a country that argues with a conscience.[14] Barack found answers in the law books and listening to the lectures and debates in the classrooms and within the law community. However, the answers he found at law school didn't always satisfy him. And often they only made him dig deeper to understand and find solutions. He also realized that, as long as the questions are being asked, what binds people together would always prevail.

In 1991, Barack graduated magna cum laude from Harvard Law School. He returned to Chicago to practice civil rights law and teach constitutional law at the University of Chicago Law School.

NOTES

1. Barack Obama, *Dreams from My Father* (New York: Three Rivers Press, 2004), 275–276.

2. Ibid., 336–337.

3. Ibid., 376.

4. Ibid., 377.

5. Ibid., 394.

6. Ibid., 429–430.

7. Ibid., 436–437.

8. Liz Mundy, "A Series of Fortunate Events," *Washington Post*, August 12, 2007, W10.

9. Jodi Kantor, "In Law School, Obama Found Political Voice," *New York Times*, January 28, 2007.

10. Fox Butterfield, "First Black Elected to Head Harvard's Law Review," *New York Times*, February 6, 1990, A20.

11. Ibid.

12. Jodi Kantor, "In Law School, Obama Found Political Voice," *New York Times*, January 28, 2007.

13. Ibid.

14. Barack Obama, *Dreams from My Father* (New York: Three Rivers Press, 2004), 437.

Chapter 5

TEACHING CONSTITUTIONAL LAW, MARRIAGE, FAMILY, AND ILLINOIS STATE POLITICS

There are times when I want to do everything and be everything. I want to have time to read and swim with the kids and not disappoint my voters and do a really careful job on each and every thing that I do. And that can sometimes get me into trouble. That's historically been one of my bigger faults. I mean, I was trying to organize Project Vote at the same time as I was writing a book, and there are only so many hours in a day.

—*Barack Obama*

In 1991, Barack graduated from Harvard Law School. Because of his position with the *Law Review* and graduating magna cum laude, he was heavily recruited by numerous law firms and also by a chief judge of the U.S. Court of Appeals for the Washington, D.C., circuit, a very powerful and prestigious position. Judd Miner, a partner in a firm specializing in civil rights cases, read about Barack in a Chicago publication and decided to give him a call at the *Law Review*. Miner was told that Barack was unavailable and was asked if he was making a recruiting call. When Miner said that he was, he was told he would be put on a list and that he was number 643.[1] Despite being heavily recruited, Barack was determined to return to the South Side of Chicago. One of his motivations in attending law school had been to gain knowledge that would make him a more effective leader. With his law degree and working in civil rights, as well as continuing to be a community organizer and representing victims of housing and employment discrimination, he believed he could effect real changes. He also wanted to be part of a community and put down roots in

Chicago. The call Miner made to Barack turned out to be quite fortuitous. After several discussions, Barack decided to join Miner's firm because he felt it fit with his commitment to community work.

After law school, when Barack moved back to Chicago, he found that the South Side had continued to slide toward decay. The neighborhoods were shabbier, the children less controlled, and some middle-class families that he'd come to know and that were part of the foundation of his community activism were moving out of the area to the suburbs. The jails were at capacity, and too many people were living without prospects, direction, or the ability to support themselves.

While a student at Harvard Law, Barack worked as a summer law associate at a Chicago law firm. There he met Michelle Robinson, a graduate of Princeton University and Harvard Law School and a practicing attorney at the firm. Michelle, a product of Chicago's South Side public schools, says her working-class parents sacrificed to put her and her brother through Princeton University. Michelle said of her parents, "I marvel at the level of commitment and sacrifice that they must have made to get us to achieve our dreams." Of meeting Barack at the law firm, Michelle said she was ready to "write him off" when she first met him. "His name was Barack Obama, and I thought, 'Well, I'm sure this guy is weird, right?'" And when she learned he grew up in Hawaii and spent his formative years on an island, she thought, "Well, you've got to be a little nuts." Barack, she says, quickly changed her mind after their first conversation.[2]

Barack was mesmerized by Michelle and vowed to go out on a date with her. According to Michelle, "He made the first move. I was skeptical at first; everyone was raving about this smart, attractive, young first-year associate they recruited from Harvard. Everyone was like, 'Oh, he's brilliant, he's amazing and he's attractive.' I said, 'Okay, this is probably just a Brother who can talk straight.' Then I heard that he grew up in Hawaii. Weird background, so I said he's probably a little odd, strange. I already had in my mind that this guy was going to be lame. Then we went to lunch that first day and I was really impressed. First, he was more attractive than his picture. He came in confident, at ease with himself. He was easy to talk to and had a good sense of humor." Michelle also says she was impressed by Barack's commitment to the community, yet for a month she refused to go out with him.[3] Michelle finally relented, and on the couple's first date they went to dinner and saw a movie. For his part, Barack says he knew almost immediately upon meeting Michelle that she was the woman he would marry. He was swept off his feet, but she needed more convincing; in fact, she thought he was too good to be true and thought about setting him up with a friend. She thought that it wasn't appropriate to date someone at the law firm she was assigned to train.[4]

Later, after they were engaged to be married, Barack took Michelle to Kenya. His family welcomed her with open arms. While there, they helped Auma, Barack's half sister, with a film project and spent time listening to Granny's stories. Barack learned that the inheritance fight remained unresolved and that, because the economy and life in Kenya had become even more difficult since his trip a few years before, many members of his family had not yet found steady work. Barack and Michelle also visited Barack's grandparents, Gramps and Toots, in Hawaii. Gramps described Michelle as "a looker," and Toots thought Michelle seemed very sensible, which Barack knew, coming from Toots, was very high praise.[5] Before they were married in 1992, Michelle's father died, as did Gramps. After their marriage, Barack and Michelle moved to Hyde Park, located on Chicago's South Side, and, in 1998, their first daughter, Malia, was born. Sasha, their second daughter, was born in 2001.

Barack had vowed when he left for law school to return to the South Side neighborhoods and effect change, and so he went to work. He was already known as a good organizer throughout the South Side through his work with the Developing Communities Project; however, not long after he returned from law school, Barack was noticed by ACORN, the Association of Community Organizations for Reform Now, one of the largest community organizations in the United States.[6] They asked him to help with a lawsuit to challenge the state of Illinois's refusal to abide by the National Voting Rights Act. At the time, Illinois did not allow for mass-based voter registration. Barack took the case, known as *ACORN v. Edgar* (Jim Edgar was the governor of Illinois at the time), and he won it.[7] In 1992, Barack became the director of Illinois Project Vote, helping register nearly 50,000 voters, many of whom were low-income minorities.[8]

In 1993, Barack went to work for a public interest law firm, where he worked as a civil rights attorney. Working on employment discrimination, fair housing, and voting rights issues, he essayed to effect real changes in the same neighborhoods where he had been a community organizer years before. While working at the law firm, he was named in *Crain's* magazine's list of "40 under 40" outstanding young leaders in the city of Chicago.[9] Barack also joined the University of Chicago Law School as a senior lecturer, teaching constitutional law. After three years of teaching and working as a civil rights attorney, Barack decided to enter politics.

ILLINOIS STATE SENATOR

In 1996, Barack was elected to the Illinois State Senate as a Democrat representing the Illinois 13th legislative district. His arrival in Springfield in January 1997 wasn't met with a red carpet or open arms. Instead, many of his fellow senators cast a rather cold eye on the new senator from the South Side. Many ensconced in the senate chamber thought of Barack as an aloof Ivy Leaguer who spent a lot of time talking about his years as a community organizer and his Harvard Law degree. Kirk Dillard, a Republican from suburban Chicago, said that Barack's Harvard Law degree and his position as a law professor made some eyes roll.[10] Some described Barack as an elitist and noted that many of his speeches were focused on policy and were highly intellectual—qualities welcomed by Barack's university colleagues but often poorly received by working-class voters, even though, during his state senate campaign, his platform included helping working families on Chicago's South Side, an area that is described by *The Almanac of American Politics* as "the nation's largest urban black community for nearly a century."[11]

When asked by Ronald Roach, in his 2004 article entitled "Obama Rising" in *Black Issues in Higher Education*, how he assessed the impact of having been a community organizer on choosing politics as a career and making a predominantly black urban community his political base, Barack answered, "I became a community organizer as a direct result of my work and study in college. I was greatly inspired by the civil rights movement . . . my coming back to Chicago, I think, opened up my potential—I consider (the experience) an extension of my college education because a lot of the things that I had read about in books I had to try to implement. It wasn't always as easy as I thought, but it also confirmed my belief in the need to give everyday folks a handle on their own destiny. And all my work since that time has been shaped by the values that were forged during those years as a community organizer." When the author asked Barack how his experience as a law professor shaped him as a political leader, Barack responded, "One of the things that an effective professor learns is how to present both sides of an argument . . . and I think that being able to see all sides of an issue, having been trained in presenting all sides of an issue in the classroom, actually helps me question my own assumptions and helps me empathize with people who don't agree with me."[12]

When Barack, a Democrat, was elected, the state capitol was under Republican control. He was known as a committed liberal and a progressive Democrat. He wrote later that he understood state politics "as a full-contact sport, and minded neither the sharp elbows nor the occasional blind-side hit."[13] Paul L. Williams, a lobbyist in Springfield, Illinois, and a former state representative, said that Barack "came with a huge dose of practicality," and characterized Barack's attitude as, "O.K., that makes sense and sounds great, as I'd like to go to the moon, but right now I've only got enough gas to go this far."[14]

As senator, Barack served on the public health and welfare committee and the judiciary and local government committees. Still in his thirties, Barack soon became a leader, developing a style that was methodical, inclusive, and often pragmatic. Working with those on the other side of the political aisle, he had a prominent role in drafting bipartisan legislation and health care reform. He also worked to make changes designed to curb racial profiling in Illinois and to make capital punishment more impartial. State Senator Kirk W. Dillard, a Republican, stated, "When you come in, especially as a freshman, and work on something like ethics reform, it's not necessarily a way to endear yourself to some of the veteran members of the Illinois General Assembly. And working on issues like racial profiling was contentious, but Barack had a way both intellectually and in demeanor that defused skeptics." Cynthia Canary, director of the Illinois Campaign for Political Reform, said of Barack, "He wasn't a maverick. There were other legislators I would turn to if I just wanted to make a lot of noise. That wasn't his style."[15] Barack worked on such issues as reproductive rights, gun control, and banning assault weapons.

While in Springfield, Barack worked long hours and was dedicated to the issues of the day. In his first two years, he introduced or was a chief cosponsor of 56 bills, with 14 becoming law. He worked on campaign finance and ethics legislation, measures that compensated crime victims for certain property losses, and on a law that prevented early probation for gun-running felons. In his third year, he was even more successful in getting bills introduced and passed. He cosponsored nearly 60 bills, 11 of which became law.[16] A major reason for his success in the senate was directly related to his ability to reach across political party lines. Over the years in the state senate, Barack persuaded Republicans to go along with many initiatives and was able to garner across-the-aisle support. Barack said of his time in the state senate that the most important thing he could do in Springfield was to bring all sides of an issue together, get it on the table, and make sure everyone feels they are being listened to. This ability, he said, was something he learned back in the days of community organizing, when he learned how to get things done.[17]

Like many of his colleagues, he also played golf, pickup basketball, and made the rounds at the parties. He was also known to join the weekly poker game with legislators and lobbyists. One of his colleagues, State Senator Larry Walsh, described him as competitive yet careful, and always hard to read. Walsh said, "One night, we were playing . . . and I had a real good hand and Barack beat me out with another one. I slammed down my cards and said, 'Doggone it, Barack, if you were a little more liberal in your card playing and a little more conservative in your politics, you and I would get along a lot better.'"[18]

Very aggressive when he first came to the senate, despite the Democrats being in the minority, Barack asked for any difficult assignments. He favored ambitious changes in campaign law, including limits on contributions. According to the director of the Public Policy Institute at Southern Illinois University, Barack's ability to work with people of the opposite party and his definite ideas about what he thought should be in campaign finance reform were impressive. He noted that Barack was always willing to recognize he wasn't going to get everything he wanted.[19]

After five years, Barack worked on what became his signature effort: a push for mandatory taping of interrogations and confessions. Opposed by prosecutors, police organizations, and the governor, Barack believed that no innocent defendant should be on death row, and no guilty defendant should be set free. The bill that Barack worked on was unanimously approved by the Illinois Senate. When the governor reversed his position on the issue, Illinois became the first state to require taping by statute. Carl Hawkinson, the Republican chairman of the Judiciary Committee, stated that Barack would always take suggestions when they were logical and was willing to listen to other points of view. Offering his opinions in a professional and lawyer-trained way, the chairman noted that, when Barack spoke on the floor of the senate, he spoke with and from conviction, adding that everyone knew that, regardless of whether they agreed with him.[20]

Barack took his legislative responsibilities seriously; however, he knew that his family always came first. In 1999, Barack missed an important vote relating to gun control. At the time, he and his family were visiting his grandmother in Hawaii for the Christmas holiday, and his daughter, Malia, then 18 months old, was sick and unable to fly. The vote was narrowly defeated, and, while his vote wouldn't have made a difference in the bill's demise, the missed vote was a factor when Barack ran against Bobby Rush, a popular Chicago Democrat, for the U.S. House of Representatives.

ENTERING THE RACE FOR THE U.S. HOUSE OF REPRESENTATIVES

From the beginning of his time in the state senate, Barack was noticed. The senate chamber's minority leader, Emil Jones, took an interest in Barack's career and sent one of his aides to manage Barack's press and strategy. By 1999, Barack made the decision to enter the race for the U.S.

House of Representatives. He'd been groomed for higher office for nearly two years, and he believed he was ready to challenge the four-term incumbent Bobby Rush. Representative Rush was a former Black Panther and a community activist well known on Chicago's South Side. Despite the expectations for higher office, the race was a clear disaster. Bobby Rush portrayed Barack as an overeducated technocrat from Harvard. And while Barack responded to Rush's cynicism about educational achievement, the question arose, for the first time, as to whether Barack was "black enough." Rush stated that Barack "hadn't been around the first congressional district long enough to really see what's going on," making racial identity an issue for the voters of Chicago's South Side.[21] Barack lost the race by a two-to-one margin. As he describes it, he took quite a "spanking" in his bid to unseat the incumbent congressman. Using a $9,500 personal loan to help finance the campaign, he found himself broke and fielding questions from the Federal Election Commission about his campaign finances. He later lent his campaign committee $11,100 more to cover refunds to donors who had inadvertently given too much. It took him two years to repay the loans.[22]

ANOTHER RUN FOR NATIONAL OFFICE: THE U.S. SENATE

After his stinging loss, Barack returned to his job at the University of Chicago and to Springfield as a state senator. It wasn't long before he grew restless in his political career, and he began having conversations with his senate colleagues about a run for the U.S. Senate. One person he had to convince about yet another race was his wife, Michelle. Her agreement and support were vital.

In mid-2002, Barack announced to his friends that he planned to run for the United States Senate. Their first question was how he would ever be able to raise the required millions of dollars, especially after the last campaign that left him paying off personal loans. According to the September 15, 2003, edition of *Crain's Chicago Business*, when Barack entered the U.S. Senate race, there was no doubt that he had "the makings of a formidable Democratic candidate—intelligent, articulate, progressive— with the potential for a strong base of support among African American voters in the Chicago area."[23] Despite these attributes, the question remained: could he raise enough money to mount the kind of statewide battle against several well-funded and better-known candidates? While in the state senate, he'd never had to spend more than $100,000 on a race. He had, in fact, coauthored the first campaign finance legislation to pass in 25 years; the bill called for refusing meals from lobbyists and rejecting checks from gaming and tobacco interests. Now in a race for the U.S. Senate, his budget called for heavy reliance on grassroots support and what is called "earned media," meaning the ability of a candidate to make his or her own news. One week of advertising in the Chicago media market, Barack was told by his media adviser, would cost nearly half a million dollars; ad coverage in the rest of the state of Illinois for a week would cost approximately $250,000. To run a race to the primary, it would cost about $5 million. If he won the primary, the cost to run a general election campaign would be another $10 million to $15 million. For Barack, this information was daunting. He tallied the amount he might expect from supporters. That came to $500,000. The question of whether he could raise the money to make a run for the U.S. Senate was a real one. For the first three months of his campaign, he and an assistant made cold calls for support. At the end of those three months, he had raised $250,000. To make matters worse, his two opponents comprised a candidate with seemingly bottomless pockets and another well-known state politician.[24]

As petitions to get on the ballot began to circulate for the March primary, Barack wasn't winning in the money-raised category; however, he was making a surprisingly strong showing in the campaign reports. Many political observers began to take notice, wondering if he could or would keep it up. By the second quarter of the campaign season, Barack had raised twice as much as one of his opponents, and only $69,000 less than the front-runner, Daniel Hynes. Noting his success, Barack said that a lot of people were surprised at his efforts and that his fund-raising had exceeded his own expectations. He felt he could keep up the pace and be competitive with the other candidates.[25]

While Barack was campaigning for the Senate, there was heated debate all across the country and within Congress and the Bush administration regarding Saddam Hussein and whether he possessed weapons of mass destruction. By the fall of 2002, most Americans were convinced that indeed Saddam had these weapons and that he had been personally involved in the 9/11 attacks. President Bush's approval ratings were about 60 percent, and polls showed that a majority of Americans were behind his call to invade Iraq. In October 2002, the Senate voted to give the president the power to go to war. At the time, Barack questioned this vote and the motives behind going to war. He felt, as most people did, that Saddam had chemical and biological weapons. He also believed, as did most people, that Saddam had snubbed the United Nations' resolutions and weapons inspectors; he also believed that the region and the world would be better off without such a vile dictator known to have killed his own people. Barack just didn't believe Saddam posed an imminent threat, and the administration's reason for going to war wasn't based on rationale that he could agree with. Barack knew that part of his campaign would include his stance on a possible war in Iraq. The question of whether he should take a position on the war was a big consideration. After all, an invasion and toppling Saddam Hussein were popular in Illinois and across the country. If this wasn't his position, if he couldn't support such an invasion, would this hurt his chances to win the election?

That same month, a group of antiwar activists invited Barack to speak at a rally in Chicago. His friends and supporters didn't encourage his attendance at such a rally; however, Barack decided he would attend. At the October 2, 2002, rally, Barack took a position on what was a popular war. To a crowd of approximately 2,000 people, Barack said, "What I am opposed to is a dumb war. What I am opposed to is a rash war . . . what I am opposed to is the attempt . . . to distract us from a rise in the uninsured, a rise in the poverty rate, a drop in the median income—to distract us from corporate scandals and a stock market that has just gone through the worst month since the Great Depression. That's what I'm opposed to. A dumb war. A rash war. A war based not on reason but on passion, not on principle but on politics."[26]

While campaigning in 2003, Barack was adamantly liberal in his views, and he continued to be outspoken in his opposition to the Iraq war. He was proud of the legislation he'd passed as a state senator, including a bill to reduce the rate of wrongful executions by requiring homicide confessions to be videotaped and another that was intended to crack down on racial profiling. He also claimed some credit for extending the life of a state-sponsored health insurance program for children and emphasized his efforts to create a job-training program for unskilled workers.[27] As well, Barack used his community activism efforts, his heritage of a black father and white mother, and being the first black president of the *Harvard Law Review* to call attention to race and to provide, for some at least, a hopeful theme of pulling down barriers and, for others, appropriate credentials for being a legislator. White liberals and African Americans listened closely as Barack spoke about issues such as jobs, health care, and education. His campaign caught fire. In the election primary, running as a black progressive in a field of seven candidates that included multimillionaire Blair Hull, Dan Hynes, the state comptroller and a member of a prominent Chicago political family, another African American, and a prominent Latino candidate, Barack won the state primary election with

53 percent of the vote. It was then on to the general election, where he would be the Democratic candidate against Republican Alan Keyes for the U.S. Senate.

RECLAIMING THE PROMISE TO THE PEOPLE: A BRIGHTER DAY—THE KEYNOTE ADDRESS AT THE DEMOCRATIC NATIONAL CONVENTION

When Barack was selected to give the speech that vaulted him into political orbit, the Democratic Party was looking for a fresh voice. John Kerry, the party's presumptive presidential nominee at the time, had met Barack twice and was impressed with his ability to connect with an audience and his smooth, methodical manner. Barack was still a state senator, but his win in the primary for U.S. Senate was considered promising, because, at the time, he didn't have a Republican opponent. Past keynote speakers included Mario Cuomo, Jesse Jackson, and Bill Clinton—esteemed company for a relatively unknown state politician from Illinois. In 2000, the keynote speech was delivered by Harold Ford of Tennessee. Ford, like Barack, was a young, dynamic African American, but, for many, his speech had fallen flat. When considering such an important speech he would give to an enormous national audience, Barack knew he wanted to deliver a speech that came from his heart, and he didn't want anyone else to write it. He wanted to have control over what he would say. Once he began writing, in longhand, while campaigning and while in his state senate office, the words came easily. About writing the speech, Barack said, "This was not laborious, writing this speech. It came out fairly easy. I had been thinking about these things for two years at that point. I had the opportunity to reflect on what had moved me the most during the course of the campaign and to distill those things. It was more a distillation process than it was a composition process."[28] Before giving the speech, Barack practiced it a few times. He'd never used a teleprompter before and had never spoken in front of such a large crowd. Once he stood at the podium, he knew what he wanted to say.

> "I was shivering, it was so good," said MSNBC's Chris Matthews.
>
> Barack ". . . electrified the crowd here," according to CNN's Wolf Blitzer.
>
> A woman descending an escalator as Barack and his entourage were ascending enthused, "I just cannot wait until you are president."

To those gathered at the convention in Boston on July 27, 2004, Barack said, "Tonight is a particular honor for me because, let's face it, my presence on this stage is pretty unlikely."[29] The enormous crowd, many decked out in colorful hats and T-shirts and adorned with campaign buttons, were more than galvanized. They were dizzy, they were mesmerized, and they were thrilled. Many asked, "Who is that tall, lanky black man?" Barack told the crowd, "I stand here today, grateful for the diversity of my heritage, aware that my parents' dreams live on in my precious daughters. I stand here knowing that my story is part of the larger American story, that I owe a debt to all of those who came before me, and that, in no other country on earth, is my story even possible."[30] At the end of his speech, the Democratic crowd was frenzied. They wanted to know more about the man, the senator from Illinois whom John Kerry had chosen to give one of the most important speeches of the convention. And many watching at home were cheering in their living rooms. Some said they stood and applauded after listening to a relatively unknown man enter the political stage. As columnist Anna Quindlen wrote in her article entitled "A Leap into the Possible," in the August 9, 2004, edition of *Newsweek* magazine, "As much of the country knows by now, the Senate candidate from Illinois is a born orator, passionate yet reasonable in a venue that seems to bring out the inner screamer in even the most seasoned politician. He galvanized a gathering long on orchestration and short on surprises. And one more thing: he revived the power and the glory of American liberalism just by showing up." Anna Quindlen also wrote that she was alone in her den, looking like a "solitary lunatic, certain that she wasn't alone in her reaction, standing up and cheering at the TV."[31]

When Barack delivered the keynote address, he was in the midst of his U.S. Senate campaign. Although he wasn't expected to win the primary election amid a field of seven candidates, in fact, he did win, and he won big, with 52 percent of the vote. However, it was the keynote address to the millions of television viewers that unexpectedly made him a national celebrity. Suddenly, there were invitations from across the country asking him to appear at campaign events. As the November 6, 2004, edition of *The Economist* described him, Barack was "the candidate America's liberal elite has long dreamed of—poised, thoughtful, eloquent, internationally minded, intellectual—and black. . . . Mr. Obama is unlike any politician to emerge in years."[32] To win the seat against the Republican candidate, Alan Keyes, Barack had to appeal to blacks and white liberals and to rural and urban voters. He also had to rise above the expectations that suddenly surrounded him. He did all of that and more. Barack's margin of victory in the Senate race was 70 percent to 27 percent. In January 2005,

Barack became the only African American U.S. senator and only the fifth in history to hold a seat in the U.S. Senate.

NOTES

1. Jodi Enda, "Great Expectations," *American Prospect*, February 5, 2006.

2. Beverly Wang, "Michelle Obama Says Husband Has Moral Compass," *Associated Press*, May 7, 2007.

3. Lynn Norment, "The Hottest Couple in America," *Ebony*, February 1, 2007, 52.

4. David Mendell, *Obama: From Promise to Power* (New York: Amistad, 2007), 93–94.

5. Barack Obama, *Dreams from My Father* (New York: Three Rivers Press, 2004), 439.

6. *ACORN: About ACORN*, http://acorn.org/index (July 20, 2007).

7. Toni Foulkes, "Case Study: Chicago—The Barack Obama Campaign," *Social Policy*, Winter 2003–Spring 2004, 49–50.

8. Ibid., 50.

9. Sherri Devaney and Mark Devaney, *Barack Obama* (Farmington Hills, MI: Thompson Gale, 2007), 36.

10. David Mendell, *Obama: From Promise to Power* (New York: Amistad, 2007), 121–122.

11. Ryan Lizza, "The Natural," *Atlantic Monthly*, September 2004, 30.

12. Ronald Roach, "Obama Rising," *Black Issues in Higher Education*, October 7, 2004, 20–23.

13. Peter Slevin, "Obama Forged Political Mettle in Illinois Capitol," *Washington Post*, February 9, 2007, A1.

14. Janny Scott, "In Illinois, Obama Proved Pragmatic and Shrewd," *New York Times*, July 30, 2007.

15. Ibid.

16. David Mendell, *Obama: From Promise to Power* (New York: Amistad, 2007), 126.

17. Ibid., 128.

18. Janny Scott, "In Illinois, Obama Proved Pragmatic and Shrewd," *New York Times*, July 30, 2007.

19. Ibid.

20. Ibid.

21. Noam Scheiber, "Race against History," *New Republic*, May 31, 2004, 21–26.

22. Christopher Drew and Mike McIntire, "Obama Built Donor Network from Roots Up," *New York Times*, April 3, 2007.

23. Paul Merrion, "Obama's Appeal Drives Cash Flow," *Crain's Chicago Business*, September 15, 2003, 3.

24. Barack Obama, *The Audacity of Hope* (New York: Crown Publishers, 2006), 110–111.

25. Paul Merrion, "Obama's Appeal Drives Cash Flow," *Crain's Chicago Business*, September 15, 2003, 3.

26. Barack Obama, "Obama '08," http://my.barackobama.com (October 3, 2007).

27. Noam Scheiber, "Race against History," *New Republic*, May 31, 2004, 21–26.

28. David Mendell, *Obama: From Promise to Power* (New York: Amistad, 2007), 271.

29. Barack Obama, "Reclaiming the Promise to the People," *Vital Speeches of the Day, City News Publishing Company*, August 1, 2004, http://elibrary.bigchalk.com (February 13, 2007).

30. Ibid.

31. Anna Quindlen, "A Leap into the Possible," *Newsweek*, August 9, 2004, 60.

32. "Obama's Second Coming," *The Economist*, November 6, 2004, 33.

This undated photo released by Obama for America shows Barack Obama and his father, also named Barack Obama. Barack's father left the family to study at Harvard University when Barack was two years old, returning only once. Barack wrote poignantly about this visit in his memoir, remembering the basketball his father gave him, the African records they danced to, and the Dave Brubeck concert they attended. Obama, then 10, never saw his father again. Courtesy AP Photo/Obama for America.

Barack Obama, holding his daughter Malia, 6, and his wife, Michelle, holding their daughter Sasha, 3, are covered in confetti after Barack delivered his victory speech in Chicago on November 2, 2004, following his race for the U.S. Senate. Courtesy AP Photo/M. Spencer Green.

Barack Obama and his wife, Michelle, wave to delegates after he delivered the keynote address at the Democratic National Convention in Boston on July 27, 2004. Some call it "The Speech," a 17-minute star-making event. Courtesy AP Photo/Charlie Neibergall, File.

Barack Obama teaching at the University of Chicago Law School. Barack arrived in Chicago in 1985 with a college degree, a map of the city, and a new job as a community organizer. When he returned to Chicago after attending Harvard Law School, he joined a small civil rights firm, ran a voter registration drive, and lectured on constitutional law at the University of Chicago Law School. Courtesy AP Photo/Obama for America.

Democratic presidential hopefuls—from left, New York Senator Hillary Rodham Clinton, Illinois Senator Barack Obama, and former North Carolina Senator John Edwards—participate in a debate in Myrtle Beach, South Carolina, on January 21, 2008. Courtesy AP Photo/Mary Ann Chastain.

Chapter 6

THE SENATOR FROM THE STATE OF ILLINOIS

Barack writes in his memoir *The Audacity of Hope* that his campaign for the Senate was indicative of some of the changes that have taken place in white and black communities over the past 25 years. Illinois, he writes, already had a history of blacks elected to statewide office and had also elected another black senator, Carol Moseley Braun, and, thus, his campaign wasn't a novelty. Barack writes that his race didn't preclude the possibility of his win, nor was his election aided by the evolving racial attitudes of Illinois's white voters. His senatorial race, he concludes, also reflected the changes in black communities.[1]

However, in Barack Obama, there was always something different and exciting; for many voters, Barack meant a change, a breath of fresh air, and a new possibility. It didn't matter to Illinois voters that Barack was a black man with an unusual heritage: son of a white woman and a black African man. Barack was an orator, a teacher, a legislator, and many gravitated to him, believing in what he had to say. To many, he signaled something new, and that was enough for them. The new U.S. senator from the state of Illinois was a celebrity almost overnight.

In the Democratic primary, Barack had two formidable opponents. One was a multimillionaire who used his own cash for the race; the other was a well-known state official. As a result, Barack was expected to lose. Instead, he won the election by an overwhelming margin. In the general election, his margin of victory was 70 percent to 27 percent—once again, an enormous victory and, for many involved in Illinois state politics, a rather surprising margin. Along with these margins, and in a race that purposely had been a clean, no-negative-advertising race with consistently positive messages, it was the keynote address to the millions of television viewers that unexpectedly made him a national celebrity.

The day after the general election, Barack was inundated with phone calls. Nearly all at once he was a political star. Senator John Kerry called. The Democratic national chairman, Terry McAuliffe, called, as did Senator Tom Daschle from South Dakota. The phone kept ringing. From within the political arena to mainstream media, people were talking. The chairman of the Democratic Senatorial Campaign Committee and senator from New Jersey, John Corzine, said, "I think Barack Obama is one of the most interesting and capable individuals that is running this time, if not in any election. Frankly, he will be one of the easier candidates to raise resources for."[2]

Yet even with all this sudden popularity, it seemed to some at least that Barack's victory, for several unusual reasons, was considered somewhat of a fluke; the contest was run like few others in history. Barack had run his race without leveling any negative ads against his opponents, and he was determined to be elected based on a clean race in which he would stay focused on the issues, resolutely stating what he thought clearly and concisely. In a primary contest among seven fellow Democrats, there weren't any negative TV ads. As well, one of his Democratic opponents, a wealthy securities trader, saw his candidacy fade when his divorce papers were made public. One of his Republican opponents, a former Goldman Sachs partner turned inner-city school teacher, was beset by his own divorce-related scandal, and his campaign never really got off the ground. Then, as a result, the Republican Party selected Alan Keyes as their candidate to run against Barack in the general election. Keyes didn't reside in Illinois and had such strict, unyielding political positions that even the most hardened Republicans steered away from his candidacy. Some media observers declared Barack Obama one of the luckiest politicians and described his run for the U.S. Senate as the easiest race in history. To Barack and his advisers and staff, this was far from the truth. They felt these pundits discounted their hard work and their consistent message, that Illinois voters wanted something different, that politics could indeed be different, and that Barack's messages of hope and common sense made a real difference. His margin of victory in the primary and the general election should have proven his points.[3] To the ballroom packed with his supporters the night of the election, Barack said, "I think it's fair to say that the conventional wisdom was we could not win. We didn't have enough money. We didn't have enough organization. There was no way that a skinny guy from the South Side with a funny name like Barack Obama could ever win a statewide race. Sixteen months later we are here, and Democrats from all across Illinois—suburbs, city, downstate, upstate, black, white, Hispanic, Asian—have declared: yes, we can! Yes, we can! Yes, we can!"[4] Indeed, the Democratic Party and many Illinois voters who voted him into office agreed.

Upon his arrival in Washington, D.C., his Democratic colleagues were beat up and discouraged. Barack's victory in Illinois, party officials said, was one of the few bright spots in otherwise difficult campaigns, and, suddenly and quite unexpectedly, Barack was a prized commodity in the Democratic Party, not only because he delivered the state of Illinois for the party, but also because he was now the only black member of the Senate. Barack, at the age of 42, swiftly felt the heat of national expectations. He didn't seem to show any of the stress and pressure when, on the day after the win, he flew around the state of Illinois to thank voters. While shaking hands with supporters that day, Barack said he thought the election signaled a maturing of not just black voters, but Illinois voters all across the board. He added that people in his home state showed that they were more interested in the message than the color of the messenger: "I have an unusual name and an exotic background, but my values are essentially American values. I'm rooted in the African-American community, but I'm not limited by it. I think this election shows that."[5]

As only the fifth African American ever to hold a seat in the U.S. Senate, Barack represented the emergence of a new generation of national political leaders. His keynote speech at the Democratic National Convention, which he wrote himself, placed him in the national spotlight. Drawing rave reviews for its eloquence and patriotic message, commentators were already calling him the first black U.S. president. Ronald Walters, a political scientist at the University of Maryland, wrote, "He was put there to support the ticket, to hit the themes, and he did his job. And on that he got, I think, an accolade of a rising star and so forth. I tend to think that speech was one that tried to identify [Obama] as a non-racial politician that tried to connect with his immigrant roots, and tried to meet the theme of diversity that was thrust upon him. It was a theme that went over great with everybody in the convention—Blacks, Whites, everyone."[6] Barack was suddenly being compared to Abraham Lincoln, Martin Luther King Jr., and Bill Clinton, and many Democrats were already wondering if he should run for president in 2012 or 2016.

The expectations were high and seemed to be getting higher by the day. Some questioned whether he would be able to fulfill the expectations suddenly thrust upon him. Donna Brazile, a Democratic strategist who ran Al Gore's campaign in 2000, said of Barack, "My greatest fear for Barack is that he'll be in the background, another black face in the sea of whiteness. For now he doesn't have to become the next black leader. He has to become a great Senator from the state of Illinois."[7] For his part, Barack was meticulous in his self-awareness and felt that the frenzy surrounding him didn't entirely make sense. At a rally for Senator Russ Feingold in Milwaukee, Wisconsin, in October 2004, Barack was enthusiastically introduced by Gwen Moore, a Democrat running for Congress: "He's all of us! He's not black! He's not white! He's not you know ... I was going to say, 'he's not male, he's not female,'" she laughed as Barack strode onto the stage wearing a black blazer and a white collared shirt as the huge crowd cheered. Squinting in the sun, Barack surveyed the crowd and said, "My wife knows whether I'm a man or a woman. I just wanted Gwen to know that." Speaking louder to the cheering crowed, he continued to say that until recently no one knew his name, and if people knew it, they couldn't pronounce it. Then, establishing his humility, he described his vision for the Democratic Party: "There is another tradition in politics that says we're all connected. I don't just have to worry about my own child. I have to worry about the child that cannot read. It's not enough that I am part of the African-American community. I've got to worry about the Arab-American family that John Ashcroft is rounding up, because I might be next."[8]

To that crowd, Barack was an everyman, and the crowd was mesmerized. People everywhere, it seemed, were feeling the same way. But what was riding on the shoulders of this tall, lanky, rail-thin man with defined facial features, a thin neck, and a smooth, articulate voice that seemed to always stay on message? People wondered: was he the great black hope? For all his brilliance and eloquence, could he really be such a huge national figure at such a young age? For some Americans, it was a confirmation that the United States was finally working. After all the oppression and divisions, here was a black man who drew votes from both blacks and whites and represented a national racial unity; the racial gap was finally beginning to close. A handful of politicians—Cory Booker, the mayor of Newark, New Jersey; Colin Powell, who once considered a run for president; Representative Harold Ford Jr., a Democrat from Tennessee; and now Barack Obama—were African Americans who, through their speech, demeanor, personal stories, and career achievements, were sharing the culture and values of mainstream America and were transcending race.[9]

By the time Barack spoke at the Democratic National Convention and after he won a seat in the U.S. Senate a few months later, some considered the expectations too high, perhaps not achievable. Yet America was now seeing a politician it had never quite encountered before. The son of a white woman and a black African man, he was black, but not quite black. He was hard to peg politically, casting himself as a politician who didn't submit typically liberal solutions to cultural problems. He said in his speech at the convention, "Parents have to teach that children can't achieve unless we raise their expectations and turn off the television sets and eradicate the slander that says a black youth with a book is acting white."[10] He argued that his party could see beyond big government: "The people I meet in small towns and big cities and diners and office parks, they don't expect government to solve all of their problems. They know they have to work hard to get ahead. Go to the collar counties around Chicago, and people will tell you they don't want their tax money wasted by a welfare agency or the Pentagon."[11]

Barack was casting himself as an unorthodox intellectual independent, closing his address to the convention and to viewers all across the country by saying, "There's not a liberal America and a conservative America . . . a black America and white America and Latino America and Asian America; there's the United States of America. The pundits like to slice and dice our country into red states and blue state. . . . But I've got news for them, too. We worship an awesome God in the blue states, and we don't like federal agents poking around our libraries in the red states."[12] The audience was thrilled; his attack didn't seem mean or cynical because it wasn't leveled against any individual. In his speech, Barack used his race to unite America. In January 2005, Barack was the only African American in the U.S. Senate, and only the fifth black U.S. senator in history. What else could he or would he do now?

TAKING THE OATH OF OFFICE

On January 4, 2005, cheered on by members of his family who had traveled from Illinois, Hawaii, London, and Kenya, Barack was sworn in as a member of 109th Congress of the United States. He writes in his memoir *The Audacity of Hope* that the day was a "beautiful blur." The sun was bright and the day was unseasonably warm as he and his new colleagues raised their right hands to take the oath of office.[13] On that day, he shook hands with Vice President Cheney and, afterward, his two daughters played on the Capitol steps. It was a day of smiles, thanks, and ceremony—warm feelings that everyone familiar with the politics of the day knew wouldn't last. At the time, the country was deeply divided on issues, including the Iraq war, immigration, education, energy policy, abortion, the environment, taxes, and the role of the courts in the legislative process. All across the United States, there was disagreement. The November 2004 election had seen the Democratic leader of the Senate, Tom Daschle of South Dakota, lose his race to a Republican and Max Cleland, a disabled Vietnam war veteran who had lost his seat in the previous election, be accused of not being a patriot. Senator John Kerry of Massachusetts and his running mate, Senator John Edwards of North Carolina, lost the election to a reelected George W. Bush. Democrats all over the country, and in the House and the Senate, were feeling bruised. The Republicans had a majority in the Senate of 51 to 48 Democrats. President Bush, feeling buoyant in his victory, declared that he had political capital and he intended to use it.

Two days after his swearing in as the freshman senator from Illinois, Barack cast his first vote to install George W. Bush for a second term as U.S. president. He immediately received his first negative phone calls and mail. For Barack, there was no notion whatsoever that his life as the freshman senator would be easy. But then Barack wasn't a typical or normal first-time senator by any means. The unusual and near constant media attention he received after his speech at the convention and his overwhelming and unexpected victory in Illinois saw to that. It seemed that everyone wanted to know what he was thinking and where he stood on issues. All eyes were seemingly on this man with an unusual heritage, a foreign sounding name, and so much charisma that he couldn't help but be noticed.

Barack had few doubts about his role in the Senate and within his own party. He knew who he wanted to be and who he could be: a force in shaping the future. In the article entitled "Great Expectations" that appeared in the *American Prospect* in February 2006, author Jodi Enda notes that in Barack there is a sense of destiny, and his background and charm, his intellect and his way with words, all mark him as someone special. She adds that he is ever mindful to show respect for his colleagues, some of whom had been in the Senate for most of Barack's life.[14] Barack wrote in his memoir *The Audacity of Hope* that when senators are asked to describe their first year in Congress, they often say it is like drinking from a fire hose; Barack says that is an apt description for his first months in the Senate. Everything, he wrote, seemed to come at him all at once. He had to set up an office, hire staff, negotiate for committee assignments, and learn about pending issues.

Then, Barack notes, there was life away from his home and family.[15] After a great deal of discussion with Michelle and other advisers, the family decided to remain in Chicago. The plan was for Barack to stay in Washington three nights per week and then fly home to Chicago. He rented an apartment and tried to settle into a more solitary, but very busy, life away from Michelle and his two beloved daughters. There were other senators with young families at home, and this common experience gave them the desire to compare notes on what works and what doesn't. As he spoke with colleagues, advisers, and new friends, comparing notes, getting advice, and making decisions, he was often told he needed to schedule time to meet with Senator Robert Byrd. Byrd, from West Virginia, was the veritable dean of the Senate and known as a passionate expert on the Constitution. At the swearing-in ceremony, Barack listened first to Senator Harry Reid and then to Senator Byrd. At nearly 90 years of age, Byrd rose slowly to speak about his many years in Congress, dating back to 1952. Barack, the new senator from Illinois, felt the full force of tradition and how not many years before, someone who looked like Barack couldn't be seated within the hallowed walls of Congress. After listening to Senator Byrd, Barack decided to unpack his constitutional law books from his teaching days at the University of Chicago Law School and reread the document. For, as Senator Byrd had said, to understand Washington in 2005 and to know what his new job as senator from Illinois meant, he needed to understand what had happened when that document was enacted and how those first debates and all the debates that followed determined where he, a black man, and America as well, was today.[16]

During the first hectic months, Barack was determined to have a focused agenda. At first, he took careful, slow steps. He turned down many invitations for appearances. He deliberately focused on several issues, such as veteran's disability pay and money for locks and dams in Illinois. He sought to demonstrate to the voters who had sent him to Washington that he was working for their interests. He also hired a knowledgeable staff, including an experienced policy adviser. Despite an experienced staff, Barack moved slower than perhaps he could have during his first year.

Author Jodi Enda, for her February 2006 *American Prospect* article, visited Barack in his office in the Hart Senate Office Building. Lining the walls, the author observed, were pictures of some of Barack's heroes: Abraham Lincoln, John Kennedy, Mahatma Gandhi, Martin Luther King Jr., Thurgood Marshall, and Nelson Mandela. She saw a White Sox baseball cap on his desk. And Barack, his long, lean frame clad in a finely tailored, charcoal-gray suit, appeared both energetic and exhausted. Following a question about the future of the Democratic Party, Barack closed his eyes and turned his face upward, as if to "contemplate the world's problems from a place deep inside himself." The question, the author noted, isn't one typically asked of a first-term senator. Barack's answer was at first typical as he listed the issues important to the party: education, health care, and energy independence. Then he said, "Where I probably can make a unique contribution is in helping to bring people together and bridging what I call the 'empathy deficit,' helping to explain the disparate factions in this country and to show them how we're joined together, helping bridge divides between black and white, rich and poor, even conservative and liberal. The story I'm interested in telling is how we can restore that sense of commitment to each other in a way that doesn't inhibit our individual responsibility, but does promote collective responsibility."[17]

A senior aide to Barack told Enda that if Barack could name one regret during his first year, it would be that occasionally he was too slow, noting that Barack regretted not signing on as a cosponsor to an immigration bill sponsored by fellow senators Edward Kennedy and John McCain. Despite his staff's encouragement, Barack felt that since he didn't have a hand in crafting the bill, he shouldn't add his name to it. After it was clear that immigration would be a contentious topic across the country and in Congress, he ultimately attached his name to the legislation, stating he wanted to strengthen a section in the bill relating to border security.[18] When Barack was asked what he was most proud of after his first year in office, he responded, "I am really proud of the work we did on veterans affairs, because it's an issue that affects people across the state of Illinois. We were able to help close the gap in disability payments going to Illinois' disabled veterans, compared to other states."[19]

One of Barack's favorite responsibilities as a senator was hosting town hall meetings. During his first year in the Senate, he attended nearly 40 of them all across the state of Illinois. After shaking hands with everyone, he listened to concerns, answering those who sent him to Washington. Barack writes in his memoir *The Audacity of Hope* that looking out at the diverse crowds—Democrats and Republicans, young and old, rich and poor—he was encouraged because he felt hope, and his time with people in his home state cleansed him and made him glad in the work he had chosen to do. He writes that sometimes, after a town hall meeting, people came up to him and gave him notes, articles, tokens, and good-luck charms, and they asked him not to change, not to be taken in by people in power; they also asked him not to disappoint them.[20]

Supporters in Illinois and around the country say that Barack often projects an "everyman" sentiment, and as often these supporters project their viewpoints onto him, saying they see themselves in him. Valerie Jarrett, a longtime friend and treasurer of his political action committee, said in February 2006 that the danger of this is that supporters assume he will do what they would do and vote the way they would vote. She adds that he has the ability to touch diverse crowds and, because of this, the expectation is that he will agree with them.[21] This universality and personal appeal keeps him from being put into a specific category. When asked whether he was a liberal, a progressive, or a centrist, Barack answered that he likes to believe he's above all that. He says, "The way I would describe myself is I think that my values are deeply rooted in the progressive tradition, the values of equal opportunity, civil rights, fighting for working families, a foreign policy that is mindful of human rights, a strong belief in civil liberties, wanting to be a good steward for the environment, a sense that the government has an important role to play, that opportunity is open to all people and that the powerful don't trample on a less powerful."[22]

While campaigning for the Senate and after arriving in Washington, Barack was often a fierce critic of the George W. Bush administration policies. He considered the Bush administration's tax cuts for the wealthy to be fiscally irresponsible. He criticized the administration for its lack of a health care agenda and energy policy. In 2002, before he announced his candidacy for the Senate, Barack spoke at an antiwar rally in Chicago, where he questioned the administration's evidence of weapons of mass destruction in Iraq. He suggested in the speech that an invasion of Iraq would be a costly mistake. He said that day, "I don't oppose all wars. What I am opposed to is a dumb war. What I am opposed to is a rash war. What I am opposed to is the cynical attempt by Richard Perle and Paul Wolfowitz and other armchair, weekend warriors in this administration to shove their own ideological agendas down our throats, irrespective of the costs in lives lost and in hardships borne."[23]

During his first year, he continued to speak out against the war in Iraq, although his speeches were more moderate. After a number of his Democratic colleagues had begun calling for a quick withdrawal, Barack told the Chicago Council on Foreign Relations that the military is a part of the solution in Iraq. He stated his support for a phased withdrawal of forces and that an exit needed to be undertaken in a responsible way, with the hope of leaving a stable foundation for the future.[24]

After the devastation of Hurricane Katrina in August 2005, Barack began to speak out more. As the only African American senator and someone who had worked on and was passionate about poverty issues, he felt it necessary to give his voice to what had happened to the region. He also knew many of the citizens living in the southern coastal areas would be looking to him for leadership. Speaking on ABC's Sunday show *This Week*, he stated that whoever was in charge of planning was detached from the realities of inner-city life in New Orleans and they couldn't conceive of the idea that people there couldn't easily leave. He later noted that Democrats, too, must accept some of the blame because they also had downplayed poverty as a national issue.[25] At the time, he also began to speak out on other issues, such as avian flu and health care costs for automakers, and he began to work on bipartisan issues, such as no-bid contracts for Katrina reconstruction projects. He traveled to Russia with Republican Senator Richard Lugar to inspect nuclear and biological weapons sites in August 2005 and then cosponsored a bill that would reduce the stockpiles of conventional weapons. As well, he encouraged members of his party to speak more about the issues typically associated with Democrats, such as energy, health care, global issues, and education. And after perhaps a slower beginning to his time in the Senate than he envisioned, it didn't take long before he was more outspoken and more active in the issues plaguing both parties and his Illinois constituents. Senator Richard Durbin, Barack's fellow senator from Illinois, said of Barack in early 2006 that there was no doubt about the future of his state's most popular politician, adding that he was an odds-on favorite to run for higher office. He also stated that if anyone wanted to invest in a Barack IPO (initial public offering), it would be a solid investment in U.S. politics.[26]

Barack also raised his standing within his party by raising money for individual congressional colleagues' campaigns and the Democratic Party. On one evening alone, he raised nearly $1 million for the Arizona Democratic Party at a dinner attended by nearly 1,400 people. He also, in 2005, raised an estimated $1.8 million for his own political action committee, known as the Hopefund. And for Senator Robert Byrd of West Virginia, first elected to the Senate nearly three years before Barack was born and who was once a Ku Klux Klan member, Barack raised $800,000 with one e-mail message.[27]

In his first two years in the Senate, Barack traveled around the world, visiting Russia, Iraq, and Kenya again. According to CNN.com, his travels were more costly to taxpayers than any other senator who entered the Senate with him. Although other freshmen members also took trips, private groups funded them; Barack does not accept such funding. In his travels, he studied such issues as nuclear proliferation, AIDS, and violence in the Middle East. Of his trip to Kenya, Barack told the Associated Press that the trip held "symbolic power" because he is the only black senator, adding, "What a trip like this does is it allows me to really target a wide range of issues that come up on the international stage and help Americans appreciate how much our fates are linked with the African continent." In Africa, Barack was treated like royalty, with crowds gathering everywhere he went. While there, he met with AIDS researchers and activists, and he and his wife, Michelle, publicly took an AIDS test, hoping to encourage Kenyans to do the same. While in Russia, he toured weapons factories and watched workers destroy explosives, and he visited sites where nuclear missiles were being dismantled. In the Middle East, he met Israel's foreign minister, spent two days in Iraq talking to officials and military commanders, and visited the Palestinian territory, Jordan, and Kuwait.[28]

Barack's travels and the issues he studied and spoke about were unusual for such a young senator, but they would not be so unusual for someone considering a run for the presidency. As well, Barack was one of two freshmen members of the powerful and highly visible Senate Foreign Relations Committee. As his first two years in the Senate came to a close, Barack was under pressure and was certainly under speculation. Would he be a candidate for the presidency in 2008? For someone with so much charm, drive, initiative, and dedication, the prospect of running for the highest office in the land, and being elected as the leader of the most powerful nation in the world, seemed like an easy decision.

NOTES

1. Barack Obama, *The Audacity of Hope* (New York: Crown Publishers, 2006), 234, 240.

2. Monica Davey, "As Quickly as Overnight, a Democratic Star Is Born," *New York Times*, March 18, 2004, A20.

3. Barack Obama, *The Audacity of Hope* (New York: Crown Publishers, 2006), 18.

4. Ibid.

5. Ibid.

6. Ronald Roach, "Obama Rising," *Black Issues in Higher Education*, 2004, 20–23.

7. Amanda Ripley, David Thigpen, and Jeannie McCabe, "Obama's Ascent," *Time*, November 15, 2004, 74–81.

8. Ibid.

9. Benjamin Wallace-Wells, "The Great Black Hope," *Washington Monthly*, November 2004.

10 Ibid.

11. Ibid.

12. Ibid.

13. Barack Obama, *The Audacity of Hope* (New York: Crown Publishers, 2006), 15.

14. Jodi Enda, "Great Expectations," *American Prospect*, February 5, 2006.

15. Barack Obama, *The Audacity of Hope* (New York: Crown Publishers, 2006), 71.

16. Ibid., 74–76.

17. Jodi Enda, "Great Expectations," *American Prospect*, February 5, 2006.

18. Ibid.

19. Kirk Victor, "In His Own Words: Barack Obama," *National Journal,* March 18, 2006, 22–23.

20. Barack Obama, *The Audacity of Hope* (New York: Crown Publishers, 2006), 101–102.

21. Jodi Enda, "Great Expectations," *American Prospect,* February 5, 2006.

22. Ibid.

23. Ken Silverstein, "Barack Obama Inc.," *Harper's Magazine,* November 2006, 31–40.

24. Ibid.

25. Jodi Enda, "Great Expectations," *American Prospect,* February 5, 2006.

26. Ibid.

27. Ibid.

28. Associated Press, "Obama Well-Traveled in Brief Senate Career," CNN. com, February 20, 2007.

Chapter 7

BEST-SELLING AUTHOR, MICHELLE OBAMA, AND ANOTHER TRIP TO AFRICA

By the time Barack was elected to the U.S. Senate, the financial aspects of his life were set; part of this financial security came from being a best-selling author. Four years after graduating from law school, he published his first book, a memoir entitled *Dreams from My Father, A Story of Race and Inheritance*. That book, written while running Project Vote in Illinois, didn't initially sell well. But after his momentous speech at the Democratic National Convention and his resulting sudden fame, 85,000 new copies of the book were sent to bookstores, and it began a climb to the top of the bestseller list.

When Barack was elected to the prestigious post of president of the *Harvard Law Review*, he was the first black student to hold the position. This gave him certain celebrity. There were stories in the *New York Times* and in *Time* magazine. There were calls for interviews and requests for him to appear at conferences. And, not unusual to someone with newfound fame and notoriety, there were calls from publishers and literary agents. What was published four years after his graduation from Harvard Law was one of many memoirs published at the time; Barack's, however, was some-what different. According to a February 2007 article in the *Weekly Standard*, author Andrew Ferguson notes that, at the time, there were many writers penning detailed accounts of their lives. By 1995, when *Dreams from My Father* was published, the author notes that bookshelves were filled with memoirs, some virtually unreadable, others good. Of the many memoirs, Barack's first book was considered better than most. But it wasn't the book he intended to write. According to Ferguson, Barack intended to write a book examining U.S. race relations and civil rights litigation, a book based on his experience as the son of a white woman from Kansas and a black man from Kenya. His experiences, and the stories he wrote about those experiences—including stories about his grandparents, childhood friends, and school and work life—kept him writing. Barack said, "Next to this human material, all my well-ordered theories seemed insubstantial and premature."[1] Sales of the book were underwhelming, and Barack later wrote, "And after a few months I went on with the business of my life, certain that my career as an author would be short-lived."[2]

Immersed in his life in Chicago after graduation, Barack worked at a law firm, taught at the University of Chicago Law School, and eventually was involved in state politics. He ran for the state senate and won. Later, he ran for the U.S. Congress and lost. And then he ran for the U.S. Senate and won by a landslide after delivering what was described as an electrifying speech at the 2004 Democratic National Convention. Once his popularity soared, his first book was published in paperback, and sales topped bestseller lists. It was because of this celebrity status and popularity that Barack was able to sign a contract in December 2004 for three more books, including a children's book to be written with his wife, Michelle. The advance for this contract was nearly $2 million, allowing him to stabilize his family's financial situation for his lifetime.[3]

Barack's second book, *The Audacity of Hope: Thoughts on Reclaiming the American Dream*, was published in 2006. This book, like his first, climbed to the top of the bestseller lists. Barack talked about the book on a publicity tour that included television talk show appearances, including an appearance on *Oprah* with Michelle. To one reviewer, the second book is closer to the book a much younger Barack Obama intended to write. According to Andrew Ferguson of the *Weekly Standard*, the second book is "high-minded and abstract, pumped with the helium of political rhetoric and discussions about policy—health care or budgeting, for example—that seem just serious enough to bore any reader except someone who knows enough about policy to find them tendentious and superficial." The author adds that the book is filled with folksiness and anecdotes and that it is only a little more memorable, though better written, than John Kerry's *A Call to Service* and George W. Bush's *A Charge to Keep*.[4]

David Mendell, in his book *Obama: From Promise to Power*, writes that the second book's content wasn't nearly as raw as Barack's first book. *The Audacity of Hope*, Mendell writes, is the work of a man in his mid-forties who by now had made concessions and reconciliations, and much of the book wrestles with how a politician can hold on to his ideals amid a forceful, ever-present press core and a media culture that feeds on personal conflicts and a political system that makes it a requirement to continually raise money. He adds that this book, from the point of view of a man eyeing the presidency, is candid, with struggles, insecurities, and failures acknowledged.[5]

The two books together tell Barack's unique story. The first book is a compelling, interesting story in the voice of the young man who is angry, funny, and a bit of a dreamer. The second is the story of a somewhat seasoned politician with lessons learned and with stories to tell from the campaign trail; it contains anecdotes about what he learned growing up and how he has applied them to who he is since taking the oath of office as a freshman senator from Illinois with an eye toward becoming the man occupying the White House. According to the reviewer from the *Weekly Standard*, "An admirer of *Dreams from My Father* can only marvel at the crudity of passages. . . . Has there ever been a better display of the destructive effects—the miniaturizing effects—of professional politics? For the only thing that separates the writer of the one book from the writer of the other is ten years of life as a politician. You're not ten pages into *The Audacity of Hope* before you begin to long for the writer of that earlier memoir—an artist, really—who never bragged of his contempt for caricature but still managed to demonstrate it on every page. Because Obama remains such an appealing figure, you want to wave him off and to thrust his own memoir at him."[6]

MICHELLE OBAMA

By the time Barack was elected to the U.S. Senate, he was a best-selling author with contracts to continue writing. The writer aspect of his life enabled him to provide financially for his wife Michelle and their two daughters. There is no doubt how important family is to Barack. As with many couples, Barack and Michelle have weathered difficult times over the years. Of the time just after their first daughter was born, Barack says, "I was just getting into politics. There were a lot of stresses and strains. We didn't have a lot of money. I couldn't be as supportive of her at home as I wanted to be . . . but she knows how deeply I love her and the girls. I try to be more thoughtful. Sometimes it is just the little gestures that make a big difference." A mutual respect is important to Michelle. She says of her husband, "He's my biggest cheerleader, as a mother, as a wife and as a career person. He is always telling me how great I'm doing. That helps keep you going when you realize that you have someone who appreciates all the hard work that you are doing."[7] Michelle Robinson Obama is described as feisty, cool, and certain. She is also said to be intensely competitive, often blunt, and always says what she means. Barack says of his wife, "She's smart. She's funny. She's honest. She's tough. I think of her as my best friend."[8]

Michelle grew up on Chicago's South Side in a small apartment behind windows and doors reinforced with iron bars. Her father, Fraser Robinson, was a pump operator for the Chicago water department, working there before and after a diagnosis of multiple sclerosis. Her mother, Marian Robinson, worked at a bank after raising their two children, Craig and Michelle. Craig Robinson graduated from Princeton and is the men's basketball coach at Brown University. Always with a competitive spirit and a commitment to perseverance and hard work—attributes she learned from her father—Michelle learned early how to be book strong and street smart. Michelle's friend, Valerie Jarrett, an executive in Chicago, said Michelle's childhood instilled in her the idea that family comes first. Michelle grew up in a family where her father and mother were ever present in their lives, not just emotionally, but physically as well.[9]

Like her older brother, Michelle graduated from Princeton University, then she went on to Harvard Law School. After graduation in 1988, Michelle returned to Chicago to work at Sidley Austin Brown & Wood, a corporate law firm. As an associate attorney, she was assigned to mentor a Harvard Law summer intern, Barack Obama. Unsure what to expect, she did wonder about the intern with a funny name who grew up in Hawaii. Barack had been much talked about prior to his arrival; the law firm secretaries gossiped about how handsome he was, and her colleagues talked about how outstanding the intern's first year at Harvard had been. Senior partners pointed to a memo Barack had written introducing himself, describing it as nothing short of brilliant. Michelle grew skeptical, recalling that the intern sounded much too good to be true.[10]

Barack quickly changed Michelle's opinion. He asked her out several times, but Michelle kept turning him down, believing it wasn't proper for her to date an employee, especially someone she was asked to mentor. She eventually relented, and the two went on a date that included dinner and a movie. Michelle was skeptical of Barack's first move, but she was soon impressed by his confidence and his commitment to community. She also liked that he was easy to talk to and had a good sense of humor. Barack knew almost immediately upon meeting Michelle that she was his choice for a spouse. According to author David Mendell, in his book *Obama: From Promise to Power*, Michelle was far less sure of Barack as a choice for a husband. He writes that his own assuredness and her lack of it say much about Barack and Michelle. Barack, he writes, is the romantic dreamer; Michelle is a balanced realist. Upon meeting her, Barack was swept off his feet, but Michelle took some convincing.[11]

In 1992, Barack and Michelle were married. A few years later, Michelle left her position at the law firm and worked for a deputy chief of staff to Chicago's Mayor Richard M. Daley. In 1993, she joined the Chicago office of Public Allies, a program that helps young people find employment in public service. Michelle's career has been a mix of public service and private practice. As the wife of a man so much in the public eye, she is both admired and criticized for having a successful career and being a working mother of two young daughters. She has said that her experiences influence her latest risky role, that of stepping onto a political ledge and into the constant, sometimes unmerciful public eye. While there is always a chance that she and Barack may slip, a chance that they may fall, in her own down-to-earth way, she says it is a risk they will take. "Our challenges get publicized, and I see that as a gift to let people know there is no magic to this." On taking a backseat to her husband's political career and his ambitions, she says she doesn't listen to critics, "I know who I need to be. I've come to know myself . . . but I'm grown up. And I've seen it up, and I've seen it down, and I know who I need to be to stay true to who I am and to keep my family on track. We don't always figure that out for ourselves as women."[12]

On the campaign trail, Michelle often tells audiences that her husband, while extraordinary, is also quite ordinary. She has the ability to humanize her husband, to make those listening to her feel that, while he is that charming, smart, cool politician with a lot to say, he is also someone who tucks their two girls into bed at night and a man who forgets to pick up his socks. She also adds that her husband isn't "the next messiah, who's going to fix it all," telling audiences that he will stumble, make mistakes, and say things you don't agree with. Sometimes, however, Michelle is criticized for being dismissive of her husband or for scaling back her career while her husband achieves his political ambitions. To this, she responds that she is well aware she can't do everything herself and also be involved in her husband's campaign; she can't hold down a full-time executive-level position and care for her two daughters while taking care of herself by exercising and eating right. She is human, she says, and she has realized that she is sacrificing one set of things for something else that is potentially very positive. That something is her husband in the White House as the nation's first African American president.[13]

ANOTHER TRIP TO AFRICA

This is where he belongs. He just goes there [the United States] to work, but he should and will come back home to be one of our own.

—a Kenyan woman

Vowing to return to Kenya after visiting there prior to entering law school, Barack went a second time with Michelle so she could meet his father's family. He vowed he would return again and often dreamed of visiting the continent as a U.S. senator. In early 2005, shortly after he took the oath of office as the junior senator from Illinois, he and his political team—including his media consultant, David Axelrod, and his chief of staff, Pete Rouse—began planning another trip to Africa. By this time, Barack's political advisers had put together a defined plan for his time in the Senate and all the possibilities beyond, including a possible run for the presidency. A trip to Africa this time wouldn't be one just to connect with his father's family. Instead, it would be as a United States senator. This heightened the awareness of the trip, nationally and internationally. The trip was a part of an evolving plan based on Barack's continually rising popularity in the Democratic Party. Within his own circle, and among the party's elite, a possible run for the White House was constantly in the forefront. Bill Clinton, still admired and even beloved by many after leaving the White House, made a highly publicized trip to Africa in 1998. As well, Robert Kennedy made a trip to Africa in 1966. While there, he forcefully denounced apartheid, sending a clear message to blacks in the United States. The images of Senator Kennedy being mobbed by Africans were seen in newspapers and on television in the United States. The similarities between Barack and Robert Kennedy, two young, charismatic, and idealistic senators with presidential aspirations reaching out to the poorest of blacks in Africa, were compelling and noted by many.[14]

The plan for the 15-day trip included visits to five countries, including South Africa and Kenya. Barack had become very popular in Africa, where he'd been adopted as a native son. His ascent in popularity and his election to the Senate hadn't been missed. To Kenyans, he was a living hero. The crowds were expected to be enormous wherever he traveled. Whatever he did and whatever he said would be noted by the media. After arriving in South Africa, Barack toured Robben Island and the prison where Nelson Mandela had spent most of his 27 years in prison. He also visited a community health center in Cape Town that treated AIDS patients. At the time, South Africa was suffering through one of the most severe AIDS epidemics in the world. Barack was outspoken in his criticism of the nation's leaders for their lack of initiatives to combat the epidemic. He announced while at the clinic that he would take an AIDS test in Kenya in hopes of erasing the stigma about the disease among Africans.[15] Barack also met privately with Nobel Peace Prize winner Desmond Tutu. Praising Barack, Tutu stated that Barack would be a very credible presidential candidate, adding, "But I am glad you are black."[16]

Michelle and their two daughters joined Barack when he arrived in Kenya. Amid songs that had been composed for his visit, many in the huge crowd that gathered at the Nairobi State House for a ceremony wore welcoming T-shirts. A group of Kenyans sang that when Barack was in Kenya, the day is blessed.[17] While in Kenya, Barack had a meeting with Kenyan president Mwai Kibaki and met with government officials and business leaders. The intensity of emotions displayed by the enormous crowds that followed Barack and his entourage everywhere clearly demonstrated that Barack was indeed a favorite son in Kenya. He had risen to power in the United States, known to most Kenyans as a great and powerful nation. This gave them all hope that, as he succeeded, so could they. It also made them feel that Barack belonged in Kenya, not in the United States.

The trip was planned to include Barack's third trip to his father's family compound in western Kenya. He had visited in 1988 and again before his marriage to Michelle in 1992. As in other African countries, in the area where his father grew up and where his family still lived, the crowds came out to greet Barack, Michelle, and their two daughters. The motorcade also included a large entourage of advisers, escorts, and media representatives. Every street was lined with waving, joyous people all hoping to get a glimpse of the senator. Barack had announced earlier that he and Michelle would take an AIDS test when he arrived in the western Kenyan province where the family farm was located. It was hoped that by Barack and Michelle taking the AIDS test in an area with a high rate of infection (second only to South Africa), many would take the test themselves.

After his AIDS test, Barack and his entourage made their way toward his father's farming compound. Near the compound, he was greeted by a group of schoolchildren who attended a school named in Barack's honor. From his donations, there were chalkboards, wooden desks, and science equipment. Because there was more work to be done for the school, Barack told the children that he hoped he could provide more assistance in the future. At the farm, Barack's grandmother, known to everyone as Granny, greeted him in front of the main house that had been refurbished with Barack's financial support. It was his first visit with Granny in 14 years. Although their visit was scheduled to last two-and-a-half hours and include a visit to his father's and grandfather's graves, due to the huge crowds and a rather chaotic atmosphere, the visit had to be shortened to about 40 minutes. Taking questions from the media as he stood with his Granny and his sister Auma, Barack told the crowd he had enjoyed a meal with his family. When the press asked if his grandmother had any words of wisdom, the answer was that Barack shouldn't trust reporters.[18] The trip to

Africa was an overwhelming experience. The crowds, the adoration, and the constant attention were intoxicating. Upon his return to the States, Barack and his team of advisers began to think seriously about a run for the presidency in 2008.

NOTES

1. Andrew Ferguson, "The Literary Obama," *Weekly Standard*, February 2, 2007.

2. Ibid.

3. David Mendell, *Obama: From Promise to Power* (New York: Amistad, 2007), 301–302.

4. Andrew Ferguson, "The Literary Obama," *Weekly Standard*, February 2, 2007.

5. David Mendell, *Obama: From Promise to Power* (New York: Amistad, 2007), 378–379.

6. Andrew Ferguson, "The Literary Obama," *Weekly Standard*, February 2, 2007.

7. Lynn Norment, "The Hottest Couple in America," *Ebony*, February 1, 2007.

8. Ibid.

9. Judy Keen, "Candid and Unscripted, Campaigning Her Way," *USA Today*, May 11, 2007, 1A.

10. David Mendell, *Obama: From Promise to Power* (New York: Amistad, 2007), 93.

11. Ibid.

12. Gwen Ifill, "On the Road with Michelle Obama," *Essence*, September 2007.

13. Ibid.

14. David Mendell, *Obama: From Promise to Power* (New York: Amistad, 2007), 322.

15. Ibid., 329.

16. Ibid., 330.

17. Ibid., 343.

18. Ibid., 365–367.

Chapter 8

OBAMAMANIA, AN EXPLORATORY COMMITTEE, AND THE ANNOUNCEMENT

This is a profoundly personal decision that I'm going through. I'm looking at the external factors: money, organization, calendar, all those things. But the most important thing I'm looking at is, Do I have something unique to bring to a presidential race that would justify putting my family through what I think everybody understands is a grueling process?

—*Barack Obama*, Chicago Tribune, *November 20, 2006*

I never had doubt about what Barack could offer, and that's what kind of spiraled me out of my own doubt. I don't want to be the person that holds back a potential answer to the nation's challenges.

—*Michelle Obama*, USA Today, *May 11, 2007*

BARACK'S STAND ON THE ISSUES

Barack's voting record was considered to be one of the most liberal in the Senate, but he appealed to many Republicans because he spoke about liberal issues and goals, but did it using more conservative language. His stand on the issues typically matched that of the Democratic Party platform, although Barack was known to be conciliatory and was always determined to reach across the political aisle for compromise, to move forward, and do what he believed was best for the American people.

According to his senatorial Web site (http://obama.senate.gov) in December 2007, Barack's stand on issues was as follows: On tax reform,

Barack believed the federal tax code was increasingly complex and unfair. Although he believed everyone should pay their fair share, reform options should focus on creating a system that was simple, progressive, and easy to comply with and without abusive shelters. On the issue of good government and responsible spending, he has worked on drafting and ultimately passing the Federal Funding Accountability and Transparency Act. On energy, Barack believes the United States must commit to a new national energy policy focusing on improvements in technology, investments in renewable fuels, and greater efforts toward conservation, efficiency, and waste reduction. On Iraq, Barack has, since 2002, continued to criticize the Bush administration's handling of the war and believes there could be no military solution. On defense, Barack stated that it was essential that our military continue to be the best in the world and that the United States must adapt to face twenty-first-century threats such as global terrorists and loose nuclear weapons. On the environment, as a member of the Senate Environment and Public Works Committee, Barack worked to ensure environmental laws and policies to balance America's needs for a healthy, sustainable environment with economic growth. On immigration, Barack shares the growing concern about illegal immigration in the United States. As a member of the Senate Health, Education, Labor and Pensions Committee, Barack was committed to providing every American with the opportunity to receive a quality education, from prekindergarten to college or vocational school to job retraining programs. On health care, Barack wrote that he promotes affordable, accessible, and high-quality health care and believes that health care should be a right for everyone, not a privilege for the few. Barack was a member of the Senate Veterans' Affairs Committee and was committed to helping the military that defends the nation today and the veterans who have fought in years past.[1]

"OBAMAMANIA": THE ALMOST SURREAL DESIRE BY MANY PEOPLE TO SEE SENATOR BARRACK OBAMA RUN FOR PRESIDENT IN 2008

From the moment he finished his electrifying speech at the Democratic National Convention in August 2004, Barack was a political star. A few months later, an overwhelming majority of Illinois voters elected him to the U.S. Senate. Naturally, there were discussions about a run for the U.S. presidency. Suddenly, Barack seemed to be everywhere, and people were talking about the tall, lanky politician from Illinois. Late in 2006, *Time* magazine had a cover article entitled "Why Barack Obama Could Be the

Next President." In November 2006, the *Washingtonian* magazine featured an article titled "The Legend of Barack Obama." In December 2006, Ken Rudin, of National Public Radio, wrote in his article "Obama, or a History of Black Presidents of the U.S." that "a quick Google search came up with no shortage of positive adjectives, everything from 'superstar' and 'rock star' to 'electrifying,'" and added a quote from a Republican operative who said Barack is a "walking, talking hope machine."[2] It seemed the country was clamoring for change, and many thought Barack Obama represented what was needed. The question was whether this change, and Barack running for president prompting a change, would be in the 2008 election or the 2012 election. Many believed the 2008 race was a once-in-a-lifetime opportunity because the nation seemed to long for a fresh face, new ideas, and a new direction. It might be the election year to run because, for the first time in many years, there was no incumbent president or vice president running for reelection; there was no lock-in front-runner for the office. If Barack waited until 2012, when he would have more experience from more time in the Senate, he would likely have to run against an incumbent president, making the race possibly more difficult.

Questions swirled around Barack and a possible candidacy. Many wondered whether he was simply a first-term liberal Democrat enjoying newfound fame. Was he truly a new brand of politics, a new sort of politician representing a change? After all, he was half black and half white; he was born in Hawaii to a white woman from Kansas and a black man from Africa—rather unique to many, an odd combination to others. Was Barack part of a postracial, post–civil rights, post–baby boom United States, and did this make any difference to the electorate? It was also noted that he wasn't a product of the civil rights movement, but rather a beneficiary of the movement. Among many voters, the question was whether he was "black enough" to earn the votes of African Americans or whether he was too black to earn the votes of white Americans. As well, many wondered whether he had the drive and discipline to survive what was likely to be, compared to past elections, a very difficult, and some might say nasty, presidential campaign.

The questions and the speculations about whether he would run and whether he was a viable candidate continued. According to a Democratic Party strategist in November 2006, Barack had yet to be tested or scrutinized, and the Republicans had yet to pore over his past. Barack would, the strategist determined, be a stronger candidate if he had been through the fire and had more experience, noting, "If he had gone from state senator to governor, and he had served one term as governor and was running for president, it would be a much more compelling case (for running in 2008). Then he would have been in a situation in which he was a final decision-maker."[3] Barack hadn't managed a corporation, governed a state, and had less than two years in the U.S. Senate. Many questioned his foreign policy credentials, a matter considered to be one of the most important issues of the 2008 election. Still, Barack was being urged to run by many who believed in him. They also believed it was a unique moment in U.S. politics and that there would never be a better time for him to pursue the office.

Barack found himself at the center of the future of the Democratic Party not long after he was elected to the Senate. He was clearly being urged, or even arm-twisted, to throw his hat in the ring. In October 2006, Barack appeared on the NBC television show *Meet the Press* with commentator Tim Russert. In an attempt to get a straight answer about whether he would run, Russert's interview went like this:

Russert:	But it's fair to say you're thinking about running for president in 2008?
Barack:	It's fair, yes.
Russert:	And so when you said to me in January [2006], "I will not." That statement is no longer operative.
Barack:	The—I would say that I am still at the point where I have not made a decision to, to pursue higher office, but it is true that I have thought about it over the last several months.
Russert:	So, it sounds as if the door has opened a bit.
Barack:	A bit.[4]

For Barack, there were other issues to reflect upon in considering a run for the presidency. While he certainly possessed many attributes—a graduate of Harvard Law School, the first black president of the *Harvard Law Review*, a state senator, a U.S. Senator, a charming, self-effacing, family man—he was also half Kenyan and half white, and many considered him too inexperienced to hold the highest office in the land. As well, he had to consider his family going through the grueling process of running for president. Did he really want to put his family through what running for political office entails? Could he and his family endure what is described as wearing an x-ray machine 24 hours per day? When David Mendell, a reporter who covered Barack's Illinois political career for several years, asked David Axelrod, Barack's chief political strategist, about this, the candid reply was that he didn't know whether Barack could handle the scrutiny, but that he knew Barack understood what it would be like. He stated that Barack was a normal man in many ways, that he loved to watch football on Sundays, that he treasured time with his wife and children, that he had an inner toughness that was reflected in the road he had traveled to get where he was, and that his struggles and challenges made him who was. He reminded Mendell that Barack was a man raised by a single mother who wasn't there to help him all the time because she couldn't be and that Barack had fought his way through many difficult times.[5]

A few days after the November 2006 election when the Democrats took control of Congress, discussions for a presidential bid began in earnest. The key to any discussion was Michelle Obama, and she seemed resistant to the idea at first. Barack said of her reluctance to get on board with him running was that together they hadn't had much peace and quiet. He added that Michelle has always had veto power, and always would, over the decisions that have direct impact on her. David Axelrod said that Michelle's veto power came into play during the weeks leading up to the decision to run. He said that she wondered whether the idea of Barack's running for president was crazy, adding that she wasn't into crazy ideas. Michelle said of her husband's possible run for the presidency, "I took myself down every dark road you could go on, just to prepare myself before we jumped out there." She wondered whether they were really emotionally and financially ready, and she had dreamed out all the scenarios she could think of. She concluded that the bottom line was that the little sacrifice they had to make was nothing compared to the possibility of what they could do if his campaign caught on.[6]

David Axelrod, who had also known Barack for several years from Illinois politics, knew that if Barack were to run for president, he would need Michelle's full support. For that reason, Axelrod brought Michelle in as a full partner to the strategy team. This meant that her voice and her opinion would matter as much as anyone else's. By December 2006, Michelle was on board, asking only that Barack quit smoking, which he agreed to do. At the time of her decision to support her husband, Michelle was a vice president at the University of Chicago Hospitals, with an annual salary of more than a quarter of a million dollars. She also sat on the board of a food supplier to Wal-Mart Stores, Inc., a position where she earned another $50,000 per year. Considering that Barack had been critical of Wal-Mart's labor practices in the past, her board seat had the appearance of hypocrisy, not something the campaign would want to deal with at any time in the future. As campaign plans formed, Michelle quit the food supplier's board and cut back on her hours at the university.[7]

And so the beginnings of a real campaign began, although by December 2006, Barack hadn't yet formally announced his candidacy. Clearly, however, he was making strides to at least test the political waters, traveling to Iowa and New Hampshire, important early caucus and primary states. On a visit to New Hampshire in December 2006, to an audience described as rock-star size, Barack said, "America is ready to turn the page. America is ready for a new set of challenges. This is our time. A new generation is prepared at lead."[8] In a *Wall Street Journal* article, author Peggy Noonan stated that Barack was "obviously planning to run." She described Barack's visit to New Hampshire, where he was greeted with "rapturous reviews, sold out fund-raisers." She wrote about Barack taping the introduction to *Monday Night Football*, where he sat behind a gleaming desk in flattering lighting, showing Barack as an actor who can absorb the script and knows by nature what a camera is. Barack, Noonan noted, has obvious appeal, has an uncompromised past, and is someone unburdened by a record and unworn by achievement. She also asked, "What does he believe? What does he stand for? This is, after all, the central question." Barack's rise in popularity, she wrote, isn't about a stand or an issue or a question, but it is about Senator Obama himself, and people project their hopes on him. When Noonan asked a young Democratic college student why he liked Barack Obama, stating that obviously Barack had little experience, the student replied that that was part of what he likes, that he's not an insider, not just a Washington, D.C., politician. Barack, the author decided, would eventually show who he is, that the man from nowhere of whom little is really known believes in the power of good nature, a need for compromise, and the possibility of comprehensive and sensible solutions achieved through good-faith negotiations.[9]

By December, despite not having formally announced a run, among the discussions and speculations, there were comparisons to other presidential races and other politicians. And while Barack's race was often discussed, his deemed inexperience to be president was also a matter of discussion. One comparison was to John F. Kennedy. Theodore Sorensen, JFK's speechwriter and political adviser, said, "He [Obama] reminds me in many ways of Kennedy in 1960. The pundits said he was Catholic and too young and inexperienced and wasn't a member of the party's inner circle. They forgot that the nomination wasn't decided in Washington but out in the field."[10] His style was compared to another former president, Bill Clinton: a natural ease with people and an ability to win people over. Like Clinton, Barack presented himself as "a new kind of politician who can rise above and bridge partisan differences."[11]

Barack was also compared to other African Americans with fame and wider appeal, including Oprah Winfrey and Tiger Woods, and to other

African Americans such as Colin Powell, fellow Illinois politician Carol Moseley Braun, Harold Ford Jr. from Tennessee, and Shirley Chisholm. But for Barack, unlike many of these other prominent African Americans, the questions included speculation about whether he could meet the great expectations, especially after his electrifying speech at the 2004 Democratic National Convention. This, to some of his supporters and to detractors, too, was one of Barack's biggest challenges. He was a celebrity candidate, and few knew what he stood for. Despite his race, his seeming inexperience, and his celebrity status, there was a clear intensity about the tall, lanky man from Illinois. "Obamamania" was rampant throughout the country, and the political and societal forces clamoring for new ideas, a new face, and politics of hope offering a less bitter brand of politics were gathering speed. In January 2007, Barack told *U.S. News & World Report*, "I think there is a great hunger for change in the country—and not just policy change. What I also think they are looking for is change in tone and a return to some notion of the common good and some sense of cooperation, of pragmatism over ideology. I'm a stand-in for that right now."[12] By this time, former North Carolina Senator John Edwards had announced his candidacy, as had Iowa Governor Tom Vilsack. And by this time in the national polls, Barack was considered in striking distance of Senator Hillary Clinton for the Democratic nomination, even though he had yet to throw his hat into the presidential ring and despite being considered the most charismatic politician to come along in years. Everyone seemed to believe his announcement was imminent. Republican pollster Frank Luntz said of Barack in January 2007, "Everyone can see themselves in Obama. He is the definition of the American dream, the definition of the American promise. . . . Conservatives see him as clean-cut and businesslike, while moderates see him as a problem solver. Liberals see him as a man from a multicultural background who breaks down racial and other barriers."[13]

THE EXPLORATORY COMMITTEE

On January 16, 2007, Barack took another step toward a presidential bid by posting a message on his Web site and sending an e-mail message to his Web site subscribers about forming a presidential exploratory committee. Addressing the message to his "friends," he wrote, "As you may know, over the last few months I have been thinking hard about my plans for 2008. Running for the presidency is a profound decision—a decision no one should make on the basis of media hype or personal ambition alone—and so before I committed myself and my family to this race, I wanted to be sure that this was right for us and, more importantly, right for the country." He went on to say he didn't expect to find himself in the position of exploring the possibility of a presidential run just a year before, but that he had spoken to so many people who were hungry for a different kind of politics. Describing decisions made in Washington during the prior six years and the problems that he said had been ignored, he said that, while all the problems facing the United States were challenging, what he considered the most challenging was the smallness of America's politics, and that is what he wanted to change first—a change of politics and a coming together around common interests and concerns as Americans. In the last paragraph of the message, Barack told his readers that he intended to file papers to create a presidential exploratory committee, and during the next several weeks he intended to talk with people around the country, listening and learning about the challenges and opportunities. He added that on February 10, in his home state of Illinois, he would share his plans with his friends, neighbors, and fellow Americans. He asked in the meantime for suggestions, encouragement, and prayers, ending the message by saying he looked forward to continued conversations in the weeks and months to come.[14]

Although his announcement of an exploratory committee was low-key, the message gained speed quickly. His supporters were eager to hear his decision, believing he was the future for America and the alternative to the status quo; his detractors were quick to note his lack of experience and noted over and over that they didn't know what he stood for. Barack's appeal on the campaign trail, his unique background, his opposition to the Iraq war, and his fresh face set him apart from the others already in the race; this, combined with the fact that many Americans were hungry for a political change, made him a confirmed top contender for the nomination.

KENYA'S REACTION TO BARACK'S CANDIDACY

Barack's decision to run for president would be no surprise to the citizens who lived in western Kenya, Barack's ancestral home. They knew their favorite son was destined for great things. Barack's grandmother, now in her mid-eighties, who encouraged his father to study in the United States, said, "I have had a dream you see, a recurring dream. . . . I have seen Barack surrounded by soldiers in dress uniform. At first I did not understand it, but now I realize it is because he is president." His grandmother added that when she first met Barack on his first visit to Kenya, she knew he was special and "praised God" that he had been able to have such a good education. "Here we all believe education is the key . . . his father had always talked about how well he was doing at school. When he came to stay with us the first time it must have been difficult, but he never let it show. He ate the same food as the rest of us, eggs, goat, sometimes fish."[15]

THE ANNOUNCEMENT

On a frigid February day in front of the Old State Capitol building in Springfield, Illinois, in front of an estimated 10,000 people, Barack told the United States, and indeed the world, that he was running for president of the United States. With Michelle at his side and his two young daughters trailing right behind, a confident Barack walked to the podium and gazed out at a crowd filled with supporters and the media, all anxiously waiting. Wearing an overcoat to ward off the stiff wind and single-digit temperatures, the gloveless Barack presented himself as an agent for generational change and as someone who intended to transform a government in shambles from cynicism, corruption, and a "smallness of our politics." He told the crowd, "The time for that politics is over. It is through. It's time to turn the page."[16]

Barack spoke comfortably to the crowd. It was obvious he was in his element, and what he wanted to say came easily and confidently. Portraying his candidacy as a movement rather than a campaign, he said, "Each and every time, a new generation has risen up and done what's needed to be done. Today we are called once more, and it is time for our generation to answer that call."[17]

While the speech galvanized the crowd and announced his intentions to the country, Barack's political life up to that point was one of charm and nearly even rock-star status. What would come next, and for many months to come, wouldn't be quite as easy and certainly less than charming. Barack's advisers and the Democratic Party, determined to run a positive campaign built totally around Barack and all he had to offer, were determined to run something other than a conventional campaign with a conventional candidate. They prepared for the many questions about his lack of experience in national politics, the level of his knowledge of foreign policy, and a past that hadn't been scrutinized or even examined. To be sure, Barack's public persona was more about his biography and charisma than about how he would seek to use the powers of the presidency. His entry into the race for president included whether, with all his strengths and limitations, he could win or whether he could even run an effective race against a political field dominated by Senator Hillary Clinton, a politician with experience in presidential politics, a command of policy and political history, and an extraordinary network of fund-raisers and advisers.[18]

But Barack spoke directly about his experience in his speech on that frigid day in Springfield, Illinois, stating that he would use his limited time in Washington as an asset and reiterating that he was an agent of change and not someone tainted by years of being a political insider and special interests. He assured the crowd and the country that he wasn't interested in politics as usual, stating, "I recognize there is a certain presumptuous-ness in this—a certain audacity—to this announcement. I know that I haven't spent a lot of time learning the ways of Washington. But I've been there long enough to know that the ways of Washington must change." Barack told the crowd that he knew his appeal would take him only so far and that his campaign was built from the ground up and that it would build and grow and give his supporters a sense of ownership in seeking a change in America. As a grassroots political outsider, he said, his cam-paign can't only be about him; it must be about the people and about what he and the American people can do together, and that together, he added, they could transform a nation.[19]

After announcing his candidacy in Springfield on February 10, 2007, Barack took his powerful voice and the message that he would often refer to as the politics of hope and began his campaign for the presidency of the United States.

NOTES

1. Barack Obama—U.S. Senator for Illinois, http://obama.senate.gov/issues (December 20, 2007).

2. Ken Rudin, "Obama, or a History of Black Presidents of the U.S.," *National Public Radio*, December 7, 2006.

3. Byron York, "Obama Madness," *National Review*, November 20, 2006, 17–18.

4. Ken Rudin, "Obama, or a History of Black Presidents of the U.S.," *NPR*, December 7, 2006.

5. David Mendell, *Obama: From Promise to Power* (New York: Amistad, 2007), 385–386.

6. Gwen Ifill, "On the Road with Michelle," *Essence*, September 2007.

7. David Mendell, *Obama: From Promise to Power* (New York: Amistad, 2007), 380–381.

8. Kenneth T. Walsh, "Talkin' 'Bout My New Generation," *U.S. News & World Report*, January 8, 2007, 26–28.

9. Peggy Noonan, "Pursuits: Leisure & Arts—Declarations: The Man from Nowhere," *Wall Street Journal*, December 16, 2006, 14.

10. Jonathan Alter, "Is America Ready?" *Newsweek*, December 25, 2006, 28–35.

11. Ruth Marcus, "The Clintonian Candidate," *Washington Post*, January 31, 2007, A15.

12. Kenneth T. Walsh, "Talkin' 'Bout My New Generation," *U.S. News & World Report*, January 8, 2007, 26–28.

13. Ibid.

14. Barack Obama, "Presidential Exploratory Committee," January 16, 2007. Personal e-mail (January 16, 2007).

15. Jonathan Clayton and Nyangoma Kogela, "Favourite Son Is Already a Winner in Kenya," *Times of London*, February 10, 2007.

16. Adam Nagourney and Jeff Zeleny, "Obama Formally Enters Presidential Race with Calls for Generational Change," *New York Times*, February 11, 2007, 22.

17. Ibid.

18. Ibid.

19. Ibid.

Chapter 9

THE CAMPAIGN FOR
THE PRESIDENCY

I like to believe that we can have a leader whose family name is not
Bush or Clinton. I like what Obama had to say.

—53-year-old retired software engineer after hearing Barack speak in
New Hampshire[1]

I think that there's the possibility—not the certainty, but the possibility—that I can't just win an election but can also transform the
country in the process, that the language and the approach I take to
politics is sufficiently different that I could bring diverse parts of this
country together in a way that hasn't been done in some time, and
that bridging those divisions is a critical element in solving problems
like health care or energy or education . . .

—Barack Obama[2]

The 2008 presidential race has been described as unprecedented and as
a history-making event. For the first time, an African American was a
Democratic front-runner with a legitimate opportunity to be the president. Senator Hillary Clinton was also a front-runner, another first in
U.S. presidential politics. There were also other firsts in this history-
making race for president: the first Mormon, the first Hispanic, the first
person to have been married three times, and a person over 70 years of age
could be elected president. After 218 years of U.S. history and 42 presidents, all white men, the field in the 2008 election included candidates
whose race, gender, ethnicity, religion, or personal history likely would
have, in the past, ruled them out from running for president. The candidates in 2008 reflected broad trends in American life that also were affect-

ing the nation's schools, work places, and neighborhoods. The civil rights and feminist movements, the influx of immigrants from Latin America and Asia, and more public discussion of what were typically prohibitive topics such as divorce, mixed marriage, gay marriage, and abortion were causing the rules to be rewritten about who could be elected president.

According to a March 2007 article in USA Today, a USA Today/Gallup Poll found that one in five Americans were "completely comfortable" with all of the breakthrough traits represented by the leading contenders in the 2008 field. Nearly a third had reservations about the candidates. The article notes that many voters wouldn't necessarily support a candidate that looks like them; that women were no more likely than men to be comfortable voting for a woman, and women over 50 were among the most skeptical of all. As well, blacks were no more likely than whites to be comfortable voting for a black, and seniors were less likely than the middle-aged to be comfortable voting for a 72-year-old to become president. Overall, the author states that four times as many Americans expressed concerns about a candidate's age than they did about race, religion, or gender. Sociologist Robert Lang, director of the Metropolitan Institute at Virginia Tech, stated that, in the United States, barriers still exist, but they don't necessarily have the same meaning as even a decade ago. "Because people are exposed to different races, ethnicities and sexual orientations in their workplace, in their neighborhoods, in their communities, they are much more comfortable . . . what used to make them raise their eyebrows now makes them shrug their shoulders."[3] A half-century ago, a significant number of Americans said in a Gallup Poll that they wouldn't vote for a generally qualified candidate for president if the candidate was Catholic, Jewish, female, black, or an atheist. According to the USA Today/Gallup Poll of March 2007, this kind of resistance had plummeted but had not vanished. Now, according to the poll, 1 in 10 say they wouldn't vote for a woman or a Hispanic candidate, and 1 in 20 say they wouldn't vote for a black, Jewish, or Catholic candidate.[4] What these opinions and poll results suggest and what their impact would be on the Barack Obama campaign remained to be seen. But with full knowledge of these trends, and with an enormous amount of personal courage and confidence, calling himself the candidate for the common man, Barack and his team moved forward.

After his announcement in Springfield, Illinois, Barack left for Iowa to jump-start his campaign. The seven Democratic opponents were formidable, and Barack wasted no time hitting the campaign trail, knowing he needed to quickly convey his message. His opponents included Senator Hillary Clinton of New York, Representative Dennis Kucinich from Ohio, former Senator John Edwards of North Carolina, who ran for vice president with John Kerry in 2004, Senator Joe Biden of Delaware, Senator Chris Dodd of Connecticut, and the governor of New Mexico, Bill Richardson. Nearly everyone in the field of candidates, except for Clinton, was deemed to have more experience in national politics, all serving in various capacities, including in the U.S. House of Representatives, the U.S. Senate, the United Nations, as ambassadors, and, in the case of Richardson, as the incumbent governor of New Mexico. Barack was determined to use all of his experience, including his years in state politics and the two years as a U.S. senator, as an asset, disregarding claims that he didn't have enough experience to be president. He was ready for the questions about his lack of foreign policy and global affairs experience; he was ready for his life and his family to be scrutinized. And he was ready to use his public persona, his eloquence, and his ability to fire up a crowd to his advantage.

Barack also knew that he couldn't use only his many attributes to convince voters. He had to have a clear message with clear answers. And he was determined to run a campaign based on hope, concentrating on giving the American people a new face and new ideas in Washington. He told the crowd in Springfield, and would tell other bigger and smaller crowds, that he knew he hadn't spent a lot of time learning the ways of Washington, but he assured everyone that he'd been there long enough to know that the ways of Washington had to change. Barack knew he had to set himself apart, and he had to hit the ground running to get his campaign off to a successful, rousing start. On the day he made his announcement to throw his hat into the ring, he left to campaign in Iowa and had plans to campaign in South Carolina and New Hampshire; all three states had early primary or caucus dates and were crucial to the path to the Democratic nomination. Before the enormous crowd in Springfield, Barack said, "It's humbling, but in my heart I know you didn't come here just for me; you came here because you believe in what this country can be."[5] This was his message at the start of his campaign. He told crowds that his campaign wasn't only about him. As someone who was a community organizer on the streets of Chicago's South Side, he understood how change begins at the bottom and grows, and that change doesn't filter down from the top.

THE IRAQ WAR, A POSITIVE MESSAGE, CONCENTRATING ON THE ISSUES

For all the candidates early in the campaign, Democratic or Republican, the Iraq war was a defining issue, and Barack spoke about it from the beginning of his campaign. In his speeches, he told crowds about his plan to end the Iraq war and reminded everyone that he opposed the war from the beginning. This stance on one of the most important issues of the time quickly set his campaign apart from his opponents, who had voted for the war authorization. Of those who had voted for the Iraq war, several were now apologizing or expressing regret for their vote. In a February 2007 interview, Barack said, "The authorization vote is relevant only because it gives an insight into how people think about these problems and suggests the sort of judgment they apply in evaluating a policy decision. There are people who sincerely believe that this was the best course of action, but in some cases politics entered into the calculation. In retrospect, a lot of people feel like they didn't ask hard enough questions."[6] He told audiences that the United States was continuing in a war that should never have been authorized and added that he was proud of saying in October 2002 that the war was a mistake. His opponents countered these statements with the fact that Barack had not given a policy speech on Iraq until he'd been in the Senate for 11 months. In response, Barack stated that, during his first year in the Senate, he took a deliberate low-key approach and didn't make any major speeches on issues that were being discussed or voted upon, stating, "As a freshman, our objective was not to try to get in the front all the time. But the truth is that in that first year, we had just seen an Iraqi election, and my feeling was that while I was not optimistic, it was appropriate to try to give the nascent government a chance."[7] Barack was also criticized for the fact that he had voted against a Senate amendment seeking to set a specific timetable for withdrawing U.S. troops from Iraq, a vote taken up by the Senate long after the authorization vote. As was often noted by his opponents, it was easier for Barack to campaign against the war and communicate his stance against the war because he wasn't in the Senate when the authorization was voted on in October 2002. When asked if senators who voted in favor of authorizing the war bear some responsibility for the war in Iraq, Barack answered that the authorization allowed the Bush administration to wage a war that has damaged national security. "I leave it up to those senators to make their own assessments in how they would do things differently or not."[8]

Barack told huge crowds at his campaign rallies that he had a message of hope, that he would run a positive campaign, and that he wouldn't resort to negativity against his Democratic Party opponents. He was determined to concentrate on the issues and communicate his message that included what he would do as president. He said he knew Americans were looking for something new and different in politics, and he assured them that he was the answer. His difference, he said, was about attitude, stressing that the bitter, decisive politics of the past could change if everyone would work together on common interests and on what concerns the United

States. He said that he wanted to unite Americans and work closely with those who disagreed with him to find common ground. This, he said, was the attitude of coming together and working together. In his book *The Audacity of Hope*, Barack wrote about his time as an Illinois senator, depicting himself as a bipartisan problem solver. "Occasionally I would partner up with even my most conservative colleagues to work on a piece of legislation, and over a poker game or a beer we might conclude that we had more in common than we publicly cared to admit."[9]

With his ideas of change, a commitment to run a positive campaign, the conveyance of a message of hope, and his stance against the Iraq war, the crowds were cheering and Barack's message was resonating. At a campaign stop in Denver in March 2007, Barack told hundreds of people that he understood they no longer had confidence in their elected leaders and that they believed "government feels like a business instead of a mission." His campaign, he assured them, was their campaign, shouting, "We have to take over Washington. At every juncture when the people decided to change this country, it changed."[10] Touching on health care, education, and energy, his biggest response came when he stated once again that the Iraq war should never have been authorized and added that the United States was less safe and America's standing in the world was diminished. A Denver man standing near the stage stated to a *Denver Post* reporter that he already knew he was backing Barack for president. "He has soul and a conscience, and he's looking out for Joe Blow." A woman in the crowd, describing herself as a lifelong Republican, said she hadn't been happy with the current administration and, after hearing Barack's speech, she liked what he said.[11] The next day, a columnist for the *Denver Post* wrote that Barack would need ongoing inspiration to keep conveying his optimism to voters and wondered whether Barack could continue to inspire after his short time on the campaign trail. In the article, he quoted a 63-year-old man who'd driven to Denver to hear Barack: "He gives me hope as a presidential candidate. He will win because the American public is ready for a change. He's energized people to a level I haven't seen since JFK [John F. Kennedy] and RFK [Robert F. Kennedy]." He wrote about a 19-year-old college student who said she wanted to vote for someone she could believe in, and of a 59-year-old woman who wanted to see Barack in person, adding that there was something about Barack that made her think she could trust him, that she thought the idea of being hopeful again was wonderful, and that she hadn't been that hopeful since 1968. The key, the columnist said, was for Barack to continue to inspire and to keep voters' attention. He agreed with an advertising salesman in the crowd: "He's timely. But as this thing goes on, he's got to get a lot more specific and a lot stronger."[12]

The sensation that was Barack Obama quickly knew no borders. While there was great interest in the 2008 presidential race throughout the world, there was particular interest in the popular young senator from Illinois. Barack was being covered by the foreign media—from Tokyo, London, Frankfurt, and Nairobi. A spokesperson for an Italian news agency stated, "Hillary and Barack are the big stars as far as the coverage is concerned. For us to have Italian journalists traveling to Springfield, Illinois, two years before the election is, by Italian standards, crazy."[13] While there was global interest in U.S. politics and the presidential race, there was perhaps a greater interest in Barack Obama because of his African American heritage, his message, and the huge crowds showing up at every venue on the campaign trail.

By the end of March 2007, Barack announced his campaign had raised more than 100,000 donations totaling at least $25 million, $6.9 million generated through Internet donations. A great percentage of the donors were first-time donors who sent $50 to $100 from home computers. Barack's campaign finance chair, Penny Pritzker, stated, "This overwhelming response, in only a few short weeks, shows the hunger for a different kind of politics in this country and a belief at the grassroots level that Barack Obama can bring out the best in America to solve our problems."[14]

By April 2007, with just over two months of campaigning, Barack was cast by many in the media as the candidate who refused money from Washington lobbyists, skillfully used the Internet to garner support and contributions, effectively used his opposition to the war, presented a genuine enthusiasm and message to successfully bring in an enormous amount of campaign contributions, and effectively used his persona and public speaking abilities to garner media coverage and support—all making him a legitimate contender for the Democratic nomination. That same month, Barack announced what he called his Five Initiatives:

1. Bring a responsible end to the war in Iraq and refocus on the critical challenges in the broader region.
2. Modernize our overstretched armed forces, building the first truly twenty-first-century military, and show wisdom in how to deploy it.
3. Marshal a global effort to secure, destroy, and stop the spread of weapons of mass destruction.
4. Rebuild and construct the alliances and partnerships necessary to meet common challenges and confront common threats.

5. Invest in our common humanity to ensure that those who live in fear and want today can live with dignity and opportunity tomorrow.

These weren't the only concerns and issues facing the United States; however, Barack knew he had to strongly show he had a firm grasp on defense and foreign policy and plainly show his strengths as commander in chief. Deflecting the criticisms of his opponents and the media, and also the concerns of voters, Barack was determined to show his strengths and send a clear message about where he stood on the important issues facing the United States.[15]

Barack's campaign was obviously gaining momentum; however, with more and constant media exposure and more people listening, with this momentum came scrutiny of his experience and countless questions about his stance on issues, his voting record, and his experience in public policy. Could he be consistent in his answers? Could he persuade the American people that he could handle being president? Could he satisfy concerns with his answers? Could he satisfy and placate voters, bloggers, and the media? According to an April 14, 2007, article in *The Economist*, while Barack had shown he could bring in campaign contributions and amass large numbers of donors, could he pass a test on foreign policy issues? During a debate in Las Vegas, Senator Edwards and Senator Clinton were each clear in their answers, providing details, proposals, and evidence of their mastery on various subjects. Barack, conversely, waffled on his answers. The questions about his performance were whether his answers and waffling were based on his inexperience or whether they were due to his known preference for giving speeches rather than detailed answers in a debate format about policy and issues.

In an effort to combat concerns about his foreign policy experience, Barack recruited highly talented, experienced, and well-known and respected individuals to advise him, including a former national security adviser and a former commerce secretary. Although he had only 2 years' experience in the U.S. Senate and 6 years in state politics, Barack had taught constitutional law for 10 years and also possessed something perhaps more important than experience: sound judgment. He argued effectively against the Iraq war in 2002 and noted that Saddam Hussein posed no imminent danger or direct threat to the United States; he warned that "even a successful war against Iraq will require a U.S. occupation of undetermined length, at undetermined cost, with undetermined consequences."[16] While Senator Clinton was clearly the front-runner in all the polls, Barack had the ability, judgment, and impressive wherewithal to put together policy statements on a wide range of topics, and he had the intelligence to not trip over details that would cause embarrassment.[17] Still, many observers were claiming that he talked in broad generalities rather than details, leaving some with the impression that he lacked the policy experience to be president.

ETHNICITY AND ELECTABILITY

The very essence of Obama's appeal is the idea that he represents racial idealism—the idea that race is something that America can transcend. That's a very appealing idea. A lot of Americans would truly love to find a black candidate they could comfortably vote for President of the United States.

—Shelby Steele, a black research fellow at Stanford University's Hoover Institution[18]

There is little doubt that in the 2008 presidential campaign ethnicity was an issue. Just a generation ago, Barack's racial heritage would be a fatal disadvantage to his candidacy. By running for president and being considered a front-runner, he was clearly making history, but the notion of his racial heritage being a detriment to his electability was a concern for the Democratic Party, his supporters, and his organization. While many Americans hungered for a change in U.S. politics and as many looked for any optimistic sign that racial tension in the United States had at least eased or, more optimistically, gone away, the question remained whether voters would elect him because he was African American. Many in the United States wanted to elect a black candidate to demonstrate to the world that there was no bigotry left in this country. Other voters supported him, obviously not concerned about his race, and still others didn't support him because he was black. But, according to a study by the Pew Research Center, Americans were ready for a black president. The study showed that 92 percent said they would be prepared to vote for a black candidate, up from 37 percent in 1958. The study also showed that white voters no longer appeared to be lying when they said they would vote for a black candidate. In the early 1990s, polls conducted just prior to elections between a black candidate and a white one typically predicted that a black candidate would do much better than he or she actually did, showing that voters said one thing but did another once they entered the voting booth. This change was clearly encouraging and to Barack's advantage.[19]

Barack was born in 1961, the year the Freedom Riders—civil rights activists who rode on interstate buses into the segregated southern states—were arrested for trespassing and unlawful assembly. The Riders were met with firebombs and riots, and many suffered at the hands of racists. The result of what happened to the nearly 450 activists during this journey was direct action in civil rights campaigns, voter registration, and the black power movement. Barack was just two years old when Rev. Martin Luther King Jr. made his historic "I Have a Dream" speech at the March on Washington, D.C. By the time Barack was seven years of age, King and Malcolm X had been assassinated and Congress had voted to protect the right to vote. Barack learned in school and from history books about these important events that helped shape the civil rights movement. When he visited Selma, Alabama, to address the Brown Chapel AME church on the anniversary of Bloody Sunday (when, on March 7, 1965, 600 civil rights marchers were attacked by state and local police with clubs and tear gas), Barack told the assembly that the event in Selma enabled his parents, a mixed-race couple, to fall in love and marry. These events and many more like them shaped the black activists and politicians that came before Barack ever entered politics. However, because he was born much later, Barack is the most prominent figure in what is now a new generation in black politics. These new black leaders and politicians include Massachusetts Governor Deval Patrick; Newark, New Jersey, Mayor Cory Booker; and former Tennessee Congressman and Democratic Leadership Council chair Harold Ford Jr. The civil rights movement opened the doors of academia, corporate America, and elite universities for this new generation. Cory Booker is a graduate of Yale Law School, Deval Patrick went to Harvard, Harold Ford went to the University of Pennsylvania, and Barack to Columbia University and Harvard Law. All these politicians and leaders and others just like them have been hailed not just as a development in black U.S. politics, but as a repudiation of black U.S. politics; not just as different from the likes of Jesse Jackson, but rather the epitome of the anti–Jesse Jackson.[20] Terence Samuel, of American Prospect magazine, wrote that Barack "is in many ways the full flowering of a strain of up-tempo, non-grievance, American-Dream-In-Color politics. His counterparts are young, Ivy League professionals, heirs to the civil-rights movement who are determined to move beyond both the mood and the methods of their forebears."[21]

Angela Davis, professor of history of consciousness at the University of California, Santa Cruz, wrote that Barack "is being consumed as the embodiment of color blindness. It's the notion that we have moved beyond racism by not taking race into account. That's what makes him conceivable as a presidential candidate. He's become the model of diversity in this period . . . a model of diversity as the difference that makes no difference. The change that brings no change."[22] Barack's racial heritage may or may not be an issue in his winning primaries in 2008 and becoming the Democratic Party's nominee; however, based on his overwhelming margin of victory in his Senate campaign to become the third black senator since the Reconstruction era after the Civil War, his ethnicity certainly wasn't an issue. In a campaign for the presidency of the United States, the ethnicity issue may be vastly different. While the 2008 campaign is historic on several levels, the change in voting patterns is enabling black candidates to make substantial rather than symbolic runs for state and national office. A report by the Pew Research Center found that "fewer people are making judgments about candidates based solely, or even mostly, on race itself."[23] All this was good news for Barack and his campaign.

Still, there was a lack of enthusiasm among black voters. One explanation was that African Americans didn't believe Barack was representative of them, being the son of a black Kenyan man and a white American woman. Many black voters weren't naturally or eagerly gravitating to Barack. Some were even stating he wasn't "black enough" to be their candidate. Barack is African and he is an American, but he isn't an African American. His ancestors didn't come to the United States on a slave ship. This sets him apart from many blacks in the United States. In April 2007, Barack appeared at a meeting of black political organizers and said African Americans "have been complicit in diminishing ourselves and engaging in the kind of self hatred that keeps our young men and young women down. That's something we have to talk about in this election." He added that he didn't want the black vote simply because he was black because that is not what America is about. "I want it to be because of what I've done, and how I've lived, and the principles I stand for, and the ideas I promote." While Barack was warmly received by this crowd of organizers, his reception wasn't a rousing success.[24]

Although Barack has said that he settled his own struggle with racial identity in his late teens and the questions about his authenticity were not new to him, he felt the debate over the issue of race was more about America's state of mind than about him and his candidacy: "I think America is still caught in a little bit of a time warp: the narrative of black politics is still shaped by the '60s and black power. That is not, I think, how most black voters are thinking. I don't think that's how most white voters are thinking. I think that people are thinking about how to find a job, how to fill up the gas tank, how to send their kids to college. I find that when I talk about those issues, both blacks and whites respond well." According to a *Newsweek* Poll in July 2007, race was no longer the barrier it once was to electing a president. A clear majority, 59 percent, said that the country is ready to elect an African American president, up from 37 percent at the start of the decade.[25]

A COMPARISON TO PRESIDENT JOHN F. KENNEDY

Another side of the ethnicity issue was whether Barack could appeal to both blacks and whites and remain true to himself and whether voters would find him authentic. As well, why was Barack able to have so much support from white liberals? The answer to this question was Barack's electrifying public speaking skills, his promise of reconciling the nation during a divisive time, and, based on his years as a community organizer and law school professor, his idealism and talent for problem solving. Along with these attributes came comparisons to President John F. Kennedy. When Barack announced his candidacy in February 2007, he was 45 years old, two years older than JFK was when he was elected president. When Kennedy ran for president, he, too, was criticized for his lack of experience and, as some perceive, for being naive and ill versed on substantive issues. The comparisons to Kennedy went further as to Barack's ability to inspire, his message of change and hope, and what some called an intellectual "coolness." Kennedy had quite a bit of experience in national politics, having served for 14 years in Congress prior to running for president, but his Catholic religion was an issue; many believe he turned his religion into an asset by his momentous speech about how he would and would not use his religion in his presidency. The issue of Kennedy's religion is likened to the issue of race for Barack. He, too, seemed to be using his race as an asset and certainly didn't ever address it as a detriment to his candidacy. Some white voters, it was believed, supported Barack because they felt voting for Barack was voting for tolerance, for a future free from the prejudices of America's past, and for the sense of hope that Barack was continually espousing, just as JFK had done many years ago.

SECRET SERVICE PROTECTION

An obvious concern for the Barack Obama campaign was security and safety. Certainly, security is an issue for any public figure; however, for Barack and his team, the issue was perhaps more meaningful. When Barack and his wife, Michelle, discussed whether he would run, they discussed the safety of the family and Barack's safety as a prominent black candidate.

Michelle Obama said many times she worried about safety and that she thought about it day and night. With as many assurances as possible and realizing it was the time and place for him to run for president, they made the decision to go forward. As many feasible precautions as possible were taken, and, in early May 2007, just three months after the beginning of his campaign, Barack was placed under Secret Service protection, the earliest ever for a U.S. presidential candidate. Although there were no direct threats, there were general concerns, including some racist talk on white supremacist Web sites. As well, Barack was drawing thousands of people at his various campaign stops, causing some to worry about his safety among such throngs of people. Democratic Senator Dick Durbin told reporters at the time that he received some specific information, some of it with a racial bias. He stated, "I expressed concern because of my affection for Barack and his family. I've traveled with Obama. I've witnessed enormous crowds."[26] In regard to race, Senator Durbin further stated, "I wished we lived in a country where that is not a problem, but it still is. The fact that Barack Obama is such a highly visible African-American candidate, I think increases his vulnerability."[27] He then approached Senate Majority Leader Harry Reid, who, along with Republican leader Mitch McConnell, went to the Secret Service and Homeland Security. Barack dismissed his own concerns about his safety in an interview in February 2007, but he wouldn't answer directly when asked whether he had received death threats, stating instead that, "I face the same security issues as anybody. We're comfortable with the steps we have taken."[28]

A HISTORY-MAKING CAMPAIGN

According to Barack's longtime political and media adviser, David Axelrod, electing Barack president would be "something you could really be proud of for the rest of your life. It would really change politics in a very positive way." Axelrod stated that he believed Barack is something different: a "trail blazing" figure who "represents the future."[29] For Barack, the campaign began as one steeped in his personal biography: that of race, optimism, natural pragmatism, and that normal, predictable, status quo political categories don't exist. For him, politics is a defining call to serve with a clear sense of mission. In his rhetoric, he invited people to believe in him. And as he made his announcement to run for the presidency and began his campaign, many asked if it was his time to run. Was he too young, too inexperienced, was he too black or not black enough? Was he for real or just another politician few could believe or support? Had enough changed in the United States for voters to elect the first African

American president? And if his supporters were inspired now, would they continue to be, and could he inspire more and enough voters to elect him to the most powerful office in the world? Although answers to these questions and many more like them could only be answered with time, there was no doubt that Barack believed what he told audience after audience along the campaign trail: "I'm fired up! I'm ready to go!"

NOTES

1. Jason Szep and Ellen Wulfhorst, "Undecided Voters Give Obama Hope in 2008 Race," *Reuters News*, November 21, 2007.

2. Eugene Robinson, "The Moment for This Messenger?" *Washington Post*, March 13, 2007, A17.

3. Susan Page, "2008 Race Has the Face of a Changing America," *USA Today*, March 12, 2007.

4. Ibid.

5. Joe Klein, "How to Build a Bonfire," *Time*, February 26, 2007, 18.

6. Jeff Zeleny, "As Candidate, Obama Carves Antiwar Stance," *New York Times*, February 26, 2007.

7. Ibid.

8. Dan Balz, "With Campaign Underway, Obama Now Must Show More than Potential," *Washington Post*, February 13, 2007, A9.

9. John J. Pitney Jr., "George W. Obama," *National Review Online*, February 28, 2007.

10. Karen E. Crummy, "Obama: 'The Country Calls Us,'" *Denver Post*, March 19, 2007, 1B.

11. Ibid.

12. Jim Spencer, "Obama Needs Inspiration to Get His Optimism Across," *Denver Post*, March 19, 2007.

13. Ryan Grim, "The Politico," *Politico.com*, March 3, 2007.

14. Jeremy Pelofsky, "Sen. Obama Nears Clinton in Campaign Money Race," *Reuters*, April 4, 2007.

15. Molefi Kete Asante, "Barack Obama and the Dilemma of Power," *Journal of Black Studies*, September 2007, 112.

16. "Where's the Beef?" *The Economist*, April 14, 2007, 36.

17. Ibid.

18. Jonathan Kaufman, "Whites' Great Hope?" *Wall Street Journal Online*, November 10, 2007.

19. James Astill, "The Campaign's Brightest Star," *The Economist*, June 16, 2007, 33.

20. Gary Younge, "The Obama Effect," *The Nation*, December 31, 2007.

21. Ibid.

22. Ibid.

23. Ibid.

24. Patrick Healy, "Obama Woos Key Blacks," *Denver Post*, April 22, 2007.

25. "Black and White," *Newsweek*, July 8, 2007.

26. "Secret Service to Watch Obama; Racism a Concern," *USA Today*, May 18, 2007.

27. "A Lot to Do with Race," *Sun-Times News Group*, May 18, 2007.

28. "Secret Service to Watch Obama; Racism a Concern," *USA Today*, May 18, 2007.

29. Ben Wallace-Wells, "Obama's Narrator," *New York Times Magazine*, April 1, 2007, 32–33.

Chapter 10

THE CAMPAIGN CONTINUES

He has staked his candidacy on union—on bringing together two halves of America that are profoundly divided, and by associating himself with Lincoln—and he knows what both of those things mean.

—*Larissa MacFarquhar*, The New Yorker, 2007[1]

In May 2007, *Time* magazine selected Barack as one of the world's most influential people. The magazine's columnist, Joe Klein, wrote Barack has "attached himself to the notion of audacity" and that it is certainly audacious for a senator with two years of service, of mixed-race parentage, and with Hussein as his middle name to run for president of the United States; and it is certainly audacious for him to challenge one of the Democratic Party's best-known and best-financed politicians, Senator Hillary Clinton. Klein said Barack's candidacy, his standing in state and national polls, and the amount of money he has raised to finance his campaign has been audacious, too.[2]

Although Barack may be bold and audacious, he's described as "cool" and informal, smooth and stylish. His rhetoric can be fiery, convincing, and, to many, very compelling. When he gives a speech on foreign policy, he often talks about alliances and how altruism must be a part of U.S. domestic and foreign policy. In a time when there are deep divisions among the American people and in Congress, Barack seeks consensus, using dialogue and negotiation to mend fences and bring people together. In the Senate, Barack's voting record is considered to be one of the most liberal, but he has often appealed to Republicans because he speaks about liberal issues and goals by using conservative language.

One of his particular abilities is that he easily, but with determination, encourages crossover appeal. At a New Hampshire event in the spring of 2007, he told the audience, "I'm a Democrat . . . but if a Republican or a conservative or a libertarian or a free-marketer has a better idea, I am happy to steal ideas from anybody and in that sense I'm agnostic . . . the number of conservatives who have called me have said, 'He's the one Democrat I could support, not because he agrees with me, because he doesn't, but because I at least think he'll take my point of view into account.'"[3] Barack is known to listen, to compromise if necessary, and to be conciliatory and bipartisan. When he speaks of poverty, he does so by not making accusations. Instead, he says, we are our brother's keeper and that caring for the poor in this country and around the world is an American tradition. When he speaks about hope and unity, it isn't just his rhetoric or spin, it is what he believes. He is committed to listening to and hearing differing points of view, and he respects the opinions of others, mindful of culture and religious beliefs.

Barack chose to announce his candidacy in front of the Old State Capitol Building in Springfield, Illinois, in February 2007. He chose the venue for reasons that include the fact he often associates himself with Abraham Lincoln. He said, "I like to believe that for Lincoln it was never a matter of abandoning conviction for the sake of expediency. Rather . . . that we must talk and reach for common understandings, precisely because all of us are imperfect and can never act with the certainty that God is on our side."[4]

If elected president, Barack would be a new face to the world. As someone who lived in Indonesia as a child, he has an understanding of Islam and could possibly bridge the gap between Christian and Muslim states. Acknowledging that the world has lost trust in America's purpose and principles, he assures voters that he would use unilateral force; however, he would seek understanding, and he would be conciliatory when it is warranted. As president, Barack says he wants health insurance for everyone, wants better schools, and wants to have the military return home from Iraq by the time he takes office. He states that he would provide visionary leadership in the twenty-first century, "a vision that draws from the past but is not bound by outdated thinking."[5]

Barack tells audiences that to renew U.S. leadership in the world, the Iraq war must end responsibly and that attention must be focused on the broader Middle East. He states that the military must be revitalized to prepare for the missions of the future and that we must halt the spread of nuclear weapons around the world and refocus efforts on Afghanistan and Pakistan—the central front, he says, against combating global terrorism. At home, Barack intends to strengthen homeland security and protect infrastructure, including mass transit, aviation, cargo, and port security. To renew U.S. leadership in the world, as president he would invest in common humanity; he writes that a global engagement "cannot be defined by what we are against, but that it must be guided by a clear sense of what we stand for. We have a significant stake in ensuring that those who live in fear and want today can live with dignity and opportunity tomorrow . . . to build a better, freer world, we must first behave in ways that reflect the decency and aspirations of the American people."[6]

> Obama has tremendous passion. I think a lot of Democrats are desperate for that.
>
> —*Iowa caucus attendee, January 4, 2008*[7]

There is no doubt that Barack has a more than plausible chance of becoming president. Since his July 2004 speech at the Democratic National Convention and after being elected to serve in the Senate as the junior senator from Illinois, his potential and popularity have grown at lightning speed. Many believe that no one in the field of candidates in either party can move an audience like Barack can. He easily uses his concise message in his oratory, telling his audiences that he's fired up, that he has a dream, and that everyone who believes and loves America can join him in changing it. With his charismatic smile, charm, intelligence, and ability at fund-raising, he is an extraordinary candidate who tells Americans that, with their help, the American dream can be restored and the country will be united again.

Barack's rise in U.S. politics has been described as the "Obama phenomenon." He's drawing massive crowds, and, according to polls, people believe in the phenomenon. However, prior to the inauguration ceremony to be held on January 20, 2009, he has a lot of work to do, including convincing not just his fellow Democrats to believe in him, but also convincing the national electorate to believe in him and his message of hope. Prior to the Iowa caucus and the New Hampshire primary in January 2008, national and state polls consistently showed him as a front-runner against Senators Clinton and Edwards; however, polls are just an estimate, based on what the experts and the media believe. What caucus and primary voters do once it is time to make their selection can't be known.

Barack's first test came at the Iowa caucus on January 3, 2008. With 38 percent of the state delegate vote in a contest that featured a record turnout of at least 239,000, Barack sailed to victory, giving his presidential campaign an early and extremely important boost. In his victory speech, Barack told the estimated crowd of 3,200, "On this January night, at this defining moment in history, you have done what the cynics said we couldn't do."[8] In the 15-minute speech, with a hoarse voice and with his two daughters and wife, Michelle, nearby, he continued, "They said this day would never come. They said our sights were set too high. They said this country was too divided, too disillusioned. We are one nation. We are one people and the time for change has come." Thanking his supporters, volunteers, and staff, he told the crowd that the time has come for a president who will be honest about the challenges the nation faces as well as a leader who will listen to the American people instead of powerful Washington lobbyists. He added, "In New Hampshire, if you give me the same chance that Iowa did tonight, then I will be that president for America." After thanking the people of Iowa, he said, "Tonight, we are one step closer to that vision of America because of what you did here in Iowa. Years from now, you'll look back and say, this is the moment. This is the place where America remembered what it means to hope."[9] The crowd, throughout his speech, applauded and chanted, "We want change! We want change!" over and over again. History was made in the Iowa caucus. A black man with a foreign name beat the field of candidates in a state that is predominantly white. He spent months getting to know the people of the state and asked that they get to know him and his message. The turnout in Iowa was driven by the young people of the state, who, in past elections, have not turned out in any great numbers, by independent voters, and by Republican voters crossing over to vote Democratic. Voter turnout also was driven by people who had never attended a caucus but who decided this year, in this election, their political participation was, at least this once, mandatory. Barack's message to Iowa was hope, dreams, and change, and he beat two formidable opponents in a pivotal state. The day after the victory, David Brooks, columnist for the *New York Times*, wrote, "Americans are going to feel good about the Obama victory, which is a story of youth, possibility and unity through diversity. . . . Obama has achieved something remarkable. . . . Obama is changing the tone of American liberalism, and maybe American politics, too."[10]

After his astounding, history-making victory in Iowa, Barack flew overnight to New Hampshire to campaign for five days for the first presidential primary to be held for the 2008 election. This was the second test of his candidacy. Barack devoted considerable financial resources to the New Hampshire primary, and, after his enormous victory in Iowa, he was buoyant and confident. The polls leading up to the vote suggested that Barack was far ahead of both of his rivals, some saying he had a double-digit lead. In fact, the numbers suggested Barack would win by a huge margin over Senator Clinton and that her campaign was facing difficulties. Massive crowds attended all his events, and, at some venues, he spoke inside to an enormous crowd and then moved outside, where those who weren't let into the venue stayed, waiting to hear Barack speak. Some predicted Barack's win in New Hampshire would seal his nomination and that Senator Clinton's campaign would be over with a second loss. However, once all the votes were counted, Barack took second in the race, with 36 percent of the vote. Senator Clinton had 39 percent, and Senator Edwards had 17 percent of the vote. Just as in Iowa, there was a record turnout of voters; Barack beat Senator Clinton among men, but Clinton bested him among women. Barack fared better among independent voters, and Senator Clinton prevailed among registered Democrats.[11] His defeat—narrow as it was, based on the number of votes that separated him from Senator Clinton—deprived Barack of undisputed momentum, something he enjoyed after his victory in Iowa. Barack conceded the race to Senator Clinton, and in his concession speech he had a new slogan: "Yes we can!" He told supporters:

> A few weeks ago, no one imagined that we'd have accomplished what we did here tonight. For most of this campaign, we were far behind, and we always knew our climb would be steep. But in record numbers, you came out and spoke up for change . . . there is something happening in America . . . when Americans who are young in age and in spirit—who have never before participated in politics—turn out in numbers we've never seen because they know in their hearts that this time must be different . . . when people vote not just for the party they belong to but the hopes they hold in common. All of the candidates in this race share these goals. All have good ideas. And all are patriots who serve this country honorably. But the reason our campaign has always been different is because it's not just about what I will do as President, it's also about what you, the people who love this country, can do to change it. That's why tonight belongs to you. It belongs to the organizers and the volunteers and the staff who believed in our improbable journey and rallied so many others to join. But in the unlikely story that is America, there has never been anything false about hope. . . . Yes we can . . . yes we can to justice and equality. Yes we can to opportunity and prosperity. Yes we can heal this nation. Yes we can repair this world. Yes we can.[12]

Despite the loss, Barack said he was fired up and ready to go, promising his supporters he was ready for a fight and vowing to take his campaign to the West and to the South, stating, "We will begin the next great chapter in the American story with three words that will ring from coast to coast, from sea to shining sea, Yes, we can!"[13]

Whether Barack will win the nomination remains to be seen. It isn't known whether whites will vote for him. And it isn't known whether he will win the African American vote. His true identity continues to be a matter of opinion. He is an African, as the son of a Kenyan man, and he is an American, as the son of a white woman from Kansas. To many of the nation's blacks, this means he's not an authentic African American. While Barack settled his own struggles over his racial identity years ago, he is careful to this day not to align too closely with the civil rights movement. He is well aware he must win the southern states, once decidedly Democratic but more recently considered a Republican stronghold. Since the passage of the 1964 Civil Rights Act and the 1965 Voting Rights Act, it isn't a coincidence that every Democratic president has been a southerner: Lyndon Johnson, Jimmy Carter, and Bill Clinton. As a general rule, successful presidential candidates must pick up the southern states, and in the past only southern "moderates" have been able to do so.[14] In order for Barack to win the Democratic nomination and win the race for the White House against the Republican nominee, he will, ironically, have to attract support from the important southern states, historically the core of the civil rights movement.

Known as the candidate of hope, Barack has declared that he is "part of the larger American story," adding, "in no other country on earth is my story even possible." When he said this the first time, he was speaking at the 2004 Democratic National Convention, and many Democrats saw him then as the party's future. Few, though, thought the future would come so quickly. Since announcing his candidacy, Barack tells his vast audiences that he intends to rise above politics and inspire hope. But hope doesn't always translate into progress or heal deep divisions. The next president who will take office in January 2009 will face many daunting issues, including a growing national deficit and trade imbalances; a stretched military that may not be able to support future commitments around the world or at home; a broken immigration policy; and a nation with the highest number of individuals serving prison sentences, with prisons being built at an accelerated rate to house them. Other difficult issues for the next president include a loss of U.S. leadership around the world and numerous social and economic issues such as health care, education, a widening income gap, and a high poverty rate.

For as long as Barack has been in politics, his approval ratings have been extremely high. Few disagree that Barack has a crowd-pleasing charisma, a lot of ambition, and an audacity of hope. And no one doubts that he is a serious candidate for president. But does he possess the nerve, a stalwart spine, and the will to do whatever it takes to succeed as president, using the best judgment to make the critical decisions in the future? At a time when America's standing in the world is strained, when the United States is mired in two wars that may not end for years, when domestic and social ills weigh heavily on average Americans, will Barack be the bridge that many say the country desperately needs? Barack has said:

> I believe it is time for a new generation to tell the next great American story. If we act with boldness and foresight, we will be able to tell our grandchildren that this was the time when we helped forge peace in the Middle East . . . we confronted climate change and secured the weapons that could destroy the human race . . . defeated global terrorists and brought opportunity to forgotten corners of the world . . . when we renewed the America that has led generations of weary travelers from all over the world to find opportunity and liberty and hope on our doorstep. We can be this America again.[15]

Crowds are turning out in the thousands to hear this tall, lanky man with a soothing, eloquent voice that inspires and exudes confidence. Sure, there are those who don't believe in him, who disagree with him, and who won't vote for him in the primaries or, if he is the Democratic nominee, in the general election. But whatever happens, because of Barack Obama, the time has been interesting, inspiring, uplifting, and, for many, something historic and possibly even redemptive.

NOTES

1. Larissa MacFarquhar, "The Conciliator," *The New Yorker*, May 7, 2007.

2. Joe Klein, "Leaders & Revolutionaries," *Time*, May 14, 2007, 57.

3. Larissa MacFarquhar, "The Conciliator," *The New Yorker*, May 7, 2007.

4. Ibid.

5. Barack Obama, "Renewing American Leadership," *Foreign Affairs*, July/ August 2007.

6. Ibid.

7. Lydia Gensheimer, "Big Crowd, Big Win for Obama in Heart of Des Moines," *CQ Today*, January 4, 2008.

8. Greg Giroux, "Obama and Huckabee Score Upsets in Iowa," *CQ Today*, January 4, 2008.

9. Jason Clayworth, "Obama Victory Speech: 'Time for Change Has Come,'" *Des Moines Register*, January 4, 2008.

10. David Brooks, "The Two Earthquakes," *New York Times*, January 4, 2008.

11. Michael Duffy, "Obama Moves On, without a Bounce," *Time*, January 9, 2008.

12. Barack Obama, "Concession Speech," http://thepage.time.com (January 9, 2008).

13. Maria L. La Ganga, "Obama Has a New Rallying Cry: Yes, We Can!" *Los Angeles Times*, January 9, 2008.

14. Nick Bryant, "A Black Man in the White House," http://newsvote.bbc.co.uk (July 3, 2007).

15. Barack Obama, "Renewing American Leadership," *Foreign Affairs*, July/August 2007.

EPILOGUE

He speaks of things that touch the heart of everyday people. We all collectively as a society have to hold onto our hope together. How else are going to make it if we don't join together to create a better society for everyone?

> —*A teacher in North Charleston, South Carolina, referring to Barack Obama after seeing him at a rally before the South Carolina primary*[1]

Something was stirring in American politics, something akin to a growing movement not seen in recent history. It was a movement that meant getting involved by answering phones, knocking on doors, wearing candidate buttons and T-shirts, and attaching stickers to car bumpers. It was a movement that included standing outside for hours in the searing heat, blowing snow, drenching rain, and frigid cold to hear candidates speak in venues so crowded that the overflow had to stand outside or in adjacent rooms. It was a movement where it was not enough to attend caucuses and vote in primaries, but it was also necessary to speak up and encourage neighbors to do the same. It meant being present and voting. It was a steadily rising movement, gaining a momentum that surprised pollsters, the media, and supporters and encouraged people who never cared about voting before. One impetus behind this growing movement clearly was a phenomenon known as Barack Obama.

To add even more to a unique and certainly historic presidential campaign, it was the young people in states across the country who were engaged, volunteering, and voting. For many of them, it was for the very first time. The February 11, 2008, issue of *Time* magazine devoted a cover story to the youth of America titled, "Why Young Voters Care Again." The article noted that, traditionally, the older the voter, the more likely they are to vote; the younger the voter, the less likely. Between 1972 and 2000, the youth vote decreased in each election cycle. However, *Time* magazine noted that while youth participation increased in the 2004 election, this year, "There seems to a youthquake. Young people sense that they are coming of age at a time when leadership—and their role in choosing it—really matters." Barack has been the catalyst, the magazine says, and also the beneficiary of greater youth involvement.[2] Barack's campaign was the first in decades to engage so many young people. In fact, his win in Iowa was almost entirely due to voters under age 25. As the campaigns moved on to New Hampshire and Nevada, it was the youth vote that helped Barack's campaign stay competitive. It was in South Carolina, on January 26, where Barack's better than three-to-one advantage among voters under age 30 more than neutralized Senator Hillary Clinton's narrower edge among those voters over age 65.

On January 27, 2008, President John Kennedy's daughter, Caroline Kennedy, wrote an op-ed piece for the *New York Times* titled, "A President Like My Father." She wrote that she had been moved over the years when people told her they wished they could feel inspired and hopeful about America in the same way people did when her father was president. This sense, she wrote, was even more profound today, which was why she was supporting Barack in the Democratic primaries. Her reasons, she wrote, were patriotic, political, and personal, and the three were intertwined; she added that the generation coming of age now is hopeful, hardworking, innovative, and imaginative, but many of them are also hopeless, defeated, and disengaged. Ms. Kennedy, a parent and someone involved in the New York City public schools for many years, stated that we have a responsibility to help children to believe in themselves and in their power to shape their future. She wrote, "Senator Obama is inspiring my children, my parents' grandchildren, with that sense of possibility."[3] Ms. Kennedy said in her op-ed piece, and as she campaigned alongside Barack, that it was her three teenage children that convinced her to support Barack. She said, "They were the first people who made me realize that Barack Obama is the President we need."[4]

In state after state, Barack has drawn more voters from today's youth than any other candidate. One reason may be that he has figured out ways to engage today's youth. In the age of YouTube, FaceBook, and other online social-networking sites, while other candidates have also used such tools to campaign, it was Barack who used them most effectively. He and his campaign team knew full well that most of today's young voters get very little of their news and information on television or from newspapers. He also knew that many go to the Internet to find information and watch speeches and news stories as they are posted on sites such as YouTube. While they may be loosely connected to traditional networks, young people are intensely connected online.[5]

Barack understood this and used it to his advantage. He tapped into the youth vote by making them one of his priorities. According to a *Time* magazine poll of Americans under age 30, nearly three-quarters of respondents felt the country was headed down the wrong track, with majorities expressing worries about jobs, affordable health care, and the war in Iraq. Their interest in this election exceeded their interest in celebrity news or sports. The poll results showed that 7 out of 10 said they were paying attention to the race and that Barack was the only candidate in either party who is viewed favorably by a majority of young people.[6] Barack's message of change has attracted many young people to his campaign. He tells young people that they can make a difference, that they matter, and that their vote counts. In the January and February primaries at least, young people were heavily involved in the campaign. Whether they would stay involved was a question that could only be answered by saying they are likely to stay involved as long as they feel they are part of something important and historic. "I am a believer that change can happen," said Patricia Griffin, 25, a student at St. Louis Community College. "So-called Washington experience has given us an unjustified war, an economy slipping, the dollar losing its value, health care impossible to afford. I'm telling my friends they can make a difference this time. They can vote."[7]

CAUCUSES AND PRIMARIES—THE ELECTION SEASON UNDERWAY

By mid-February, after 10 Democratic primaries and caucuses, 8 of which had both Democrats and Republicans competing on the same day, it was Democratic voters who were setting turnout records. Enthusiasm on the Democratic side of the ballot was high and getting higher. Democratic voters were clearly excited, and the leaders of the Democratic Party were elated at the overall energy among voters.

After a great deal of anticipation among voters and elected officials, and with an immense amount of media buildup and hype, the voting season began in earnest just after the new year. The first contest was the Iowa caucus held on January 3, 2008. With a record turnout of Democratic voters that astonished even the most skeptical, Barack shocked the media and voters across the nation by not only winning, but winning by a huge margin. The next contest was the New Hampshire primary, held on January 8. Nearly 290,000 people voted in New Hampshire, a number well above the Republican and the Democratic turnout in the prior election. While Barack won 36 percent of the vote, Senator Hillary Clinton won the primary with 39 percent of the total votes cast. The candidates then moved to the Nevada caucus held on January 19. In a state where the union vote and the Hispanic vote were represented in big numbers, more than 117,000 voted compared to the 9,000 that participated in 2004.[8] In this contest, Clinton won 51 percent of the vote, to Barack's 45 percent.[9] The race then moved to South Carolina on January 25, 2008. Voters, especially African American voters, came out in droves to see and hear Barack convey his message of hope and change to all the voters of the state. They came to packed venues, not just for a glimpse of the first black candidate with a serious chance at winning the White House, but also because they were drawn by Barack's message of bringing Americans of all backgrounds together.

Barack and his advisers knew that he needed to win in South Carolina or at the very least to show to all voters that his Iowa win was not a fluke. Resoundingly, Barack won with 55 percent of the vote, doubling Clinton's share.[10] According to exit polling, Barack took 80 percent of the vote among black voters, a group that made up just more than half of all voters in the state. The overall turnout proved that Democratic voters appeared to be much more motivated thus far in the presidential race than Republican voters. The total turnout of approximately 532,000 voters in the Democratic primary greatly exceeded the unofficial voter total of roughly 444,000 in the Republican primary held the prior Saturday. In all, the Democratic vote was 80 percent over the turnout for the 2004 Democratic primary, and Barack's vote count narrowly exceeded the total votes cast for all of the candidates in the 2004 primary.[11] This huge win was the second for Barack, and many across America came to believe his campaign was a genuine and realistic run for the highest office in the land.

In his victory speech, Barack told the enormous crowd of clapping, shouting supporters that the choice in the election was not between regions, religions, or genders, or rich versus poor, young versus old; and it was not about black or white. He said it was about not settling for the same divisions and distractions and drama that pass for politics, but about whether the country reaches for a politics of common sense and innovation, a politics, he said, of shared sacrifice and shared prosperity.[12] For Barack Obama and his supporters, the campaign now took on a greater momentum than ever before.

The campaign moved on to what was commonly called Super Tuesday, February 5, when more than 20 states held either a primary or caucus event. With more than 2,000 delegates at stake, including such delegate-rich states as California with 441 delegates, Illinois with 185, and New York with 281 delegates, Super Tuesday was as close as it could be to a national presidential primary. When all votes were tallied, Barack won more individual states with 13, including his home state of Illinois; Clinton won 8 states, including her adopted home state of New York, and California, which gave her more delegates than Barack. The popular vote from Super Tuesday made for a very close race. According to an analysis by the *New York Times*, Clinton won 7,427,700 votes, or 50.20 percent of the vote, and Barack won 7,369,798 votes, or 49.80 percent.[13] Exit polling suggested that Barack did well with African Americans, men, the wealthy, voters with college degrees, and those voters considered to be liberal. Barack also did well among young people. These polls also showed Clinton did well with women, older voters, Latinos, and those with less education and lower incomes.[14] With more evidence that the Democrats had the motivation and energy and that voters were inspired enough by their candidates to be involved in primaries and caucuses, on Super Tuesday, at least 15,417,521 voted Democratic and 9,181,297 voted Republican.[15] After Super Tuesday, Clinton and Barack were in a dead heat for the nomination.

The next events were in Nebraska, Washington State, the Virgin Islands, and Louisiana on February 9. As with all the previous contests, excitement ran high, and the turnout was record-breaking. In Nebraska, organizers at two caucus sites were so overrun by crowds they abandoned the traditional caucusing procedures and used scrap-paper ballots instead. One county reported that traffic was backed up as thousands of voters showed up at a precinct where organizers had planned for only hundreds. In Washington State, it was reported that the turnout was nearly double what it was in 2004.[16] With 203 delegates at stake, Barack swept all four contests, garnering twice the number of votes in Washington and Nebraska as Clinton, and winning Louisiana with 57 percent of the vote versus Clinton's 36 percent. In the Virgin Islands, Barack won 90 percent of the vote, to Clinton's 8 percent. Needless to say, it was a very good weekend for Barack and his energized supporters.

The next contests, known as the Potomac Primaries, were in Washington, D.C., Maryland, and Virginia. For Barack, each of these states was important because he had previous success among African American voters, and these states featured large African American communities; these states also had significant numbers of affluent, highly educated voters, a voting segment from which Barack had drawn support in prior contests. When all votes were tallied, Barack won big, sweeping all three states. In Washington, D.C., Barack had 75 percent of the vote, versus Clinton's 24 percent. In Maryland, the results were Barack at 60 percent and Clinton with 37 percent. In Virginia, Barack won 64 percent of the vote, and Clinton won 35 percent.[17] Rolling to victory, Barack extended his winning streak to nine Democratic nominating contests. As well, the outcome in these states provided Barack with the ability to unequivocally assert that the race was indeed breaking his way. According to an analysis by the *New York Times*, Barack demonstrated impressive strength among not only groups that backed him in earlier primaries and caucuses—African Americans, younger voters, high-income voters, and independents—but also drew votes from older voters, women, and lower-income people, which had been Clinton's base of support all along. According to exit polls, Barack also won majorities of white men and Hispanic voters in Virginia.[18]

On February 19, the race moved on to the Wisconsin primary, where there were 121 delegates at stake, and to the Hawaii caucus with 20 delegates. To no one's surprise, Barack won the Hawaii caucus, in the state where he grew up and was known as a favorite son, 76 percent to Clinton's 24 percent. In Wisconsin, Barack won 58 percent of the vote, to Clinton's 41 percent.[19] For Barack and his supporters, the momentum was evident, but all eyes were on the next primaries on March 4, another Tuesday rich with delegates, much like the Super Tuesday contests held in early February; and it was another Tuesday with crucial contests for both candidates. While Barack was confident and had the momentum, most political pundits agreed that out of the four states holding primaries, Texas, Ohio, Vermont, and Rhode Island, Clinton was favored to win in Texas, with 193 delegates, and Ohio, with 141 delegates. Barack took his campaign to all four states and spent heavily on ads in Texas and Ohio. When all votes were counted, Barack won Vermont by 30 points. Clinton won the other three states, Texas by 4 points, Rhode Island by 18 points, and Ohio by 10 points.

Barack's winning streak was snapped. To his supporters that night, he said they should settle in for a long fight for the Democratic presidential nomination, stating, "What my head tells me is that we've got a very sizable delegate lead that is going to be hard to overcome. But, look, she is a tenacious and determined candidate, so we're just going to make sure we work as hard as we can, as long as it takes. . . . No matter what happens tonight, we have the same delegate lead as we had this morning, we are on our way to winning this nomination." Clinton gained momentum from her big wins, even though she gained little in delegate count and in the total popular vote. Speaking to a cheering crowd in Columbus, Ohio, she said, "For everyone who has been counted out but refused to be knocked out, for everyone who has stumbled but stood right back up and for everyone who works hard and never gives up—this one is for you. You know what they say—as Ohio goes, so goes the nation. This nation is coming back and so is this campaign. People of Ohio have said it loudly and clearly: We're going on, we're going strong, and we're going all the way."[20] Clinton stated that she demonstrated her general-election strength by winning primaries in the big states Democrats would need to count on in the fall, including the states she had won in previous primaries in California, New York, and New Jersey. Despite her wins, poll results in Texas and Ohio showed that a majority of voters said they thought Barack was more likely to beat the Republican nominee in the November election.[21]

The next contest was in Wyoming on March 8, 2008, for 18 delegates. Barack won with 61 percent to Clinton's 38 percent. On March 11, Mississippi held its primary, where there were 40 delegates at stake; Barack won that contest 61 percent to Clinton's 37 percent. With that win, Barack had won 27 states and Clinton 16 states; despite Barack's margin, the delegate count and total number of popular votes did not give a clear winner. The race would continue to the next primaries, including the Pennsylvania contest on April 22, 2008, and nine more primaries in May and June.

SUPERDELEGATES AND THE MICHIGAN AND FLORIDA PRIMARIES

At the beginning of April 2008, the race for the Democratic nomination remained very tight; neither Barack nor Hillary had enough delegates to secure the nomination and it didn't appear that either of them would be able to garner enough delegates in future primaries and caucuses to win the nomination prior to the convention in August 2008. Discussions in both camps and by the political pundits turned to the Superdelegates, those elected and party officials who may have the task of deciding the Democratic nominee at the convention. According to the *New York Times*, as of April 4, 2008, of the 714 Superdelegates, 220 supported Barack, 257 supported Hillary, with the remaining 242 listed as preferences unknown.[22] Since Super Tuesday (the February 5, 2008 primaries, collectively), 68 Superdelegates declared their support for Barack. According to figures from Barack's campaign that Hillary's aides had not disputed, Hillary had seen a net loss of two Superdelegates. At this point,

Hillary trailed Barack by more than 160 pledged delegates, which are those chosen in state primaries or caucuses. Hillary was making a concerted effort to persuade the still-uncommitted Superdelegates to back her and her campaign, or to continue not pledging support so that her campaign had a chance to demonstrate momentum and superior electability in the upcoming primaries (Pennsylvania primary on April 22, through the Montana and South Dakota primaries on June 3, 2008).[23]

Another matter permeated the news during this time: whether the Michigan and Florida delegates would be seated at the Democratic National Convention to cast their state's delegate votes. The Democratic Party had stripped Florida and Michigan of their delegates for violating Democratic Party rules by holding their primaries too early. Both Barack and Hillary had agreed not to campaign in either state. In Michigan, Barack had withdrawn his name from the ballot; Hillary's name remained. Hillary did not campaign in Florida, but she did have fund-raising events there while Barack did not campaign or hold fund-raising events in the state. Since she won in both states, if the votes were counted, Hillary would increase her total number of delegates, bringing her closer to Barack's total in both the popular vote and delegate count. Plus, she could claim she had won two more large, delegate-rich states and could also claim to voters and the Superdelegates that she had a better chance of beating the Republican nominee, John McCain, in the general election.

Both Hillary and her campaign were pushing for the votes to count and for the delegates to be seated at the convention. Barack wanted the delegation to be seated at the convention, however, he stated he would stand by the agreement he made with the Democratic Party not to campaign in either state, based on the state's decision to violate the rules and hold early primaries. As of the beginning of April 2008, no decisions had been made as to what to do with the Florida and Michigan votes. It appeared that neither of the states would have another primary; nor would the votes cast be counted in either the popular vote total or in the number of delegates pledged to each candidate.

Hillary vowed to continue the race until the convention, despite some calls for her to end her campaign. She stated that she had won in states Democrats need in order to win the White House and that she didn't believe the voters in all the primaries and caucuses to date would want her to drop out of the race. As of early April, there were more contests remaining and she wanted to take her campaign all the way to the Democratic convention in Denver in August. In an early April telephone interview with Mark Halperin of *Time* magazine, he asked Hillary if she was comfortable with the fact that the only way she could win the nomination is at the Democratic convention with the Superdelegates casting their votes and thereby electing the party's nominee. She responded, "Neither of us will reach the number of delegates needed. And all delegates have to assess who they think will be the strongest nominee against [John] McCain and who they believe would do the best job. . . . From my perspective, those are all very legitimate questions, and every delegate, with very few exceptions, is free to make up his or her mind . . . every delegate is expected to exercise independent judgment."[24]

Both Barack and Hillary continued to campaign and prepare for the primary and caucus contests in eight states and in Guam and Puerto Rico, for a total of 674 total delegates at stake. Just prior to the April 22 primary in Pennsylvania, with 188 delegates at stake, Hillary was maintaining a lead in the polls. According to *Time* magazine's Web site *thepage.com*, on April 8, 2008, a Quinnipiac University poll conducted between April 3 and 6—noting a margin of error of 2.7 points—showed Hillary led Barack by 6 points. Both candidates were well aware that a win in Pennsylvania was crucial. For Barack, it would mean continued momentum and the possibility of additional Superdelegates pledging their support. It would also prove he is the best candidate to be the party's nominee and the candidate who would win the general election against John McCain. For Hillary, it would mean she had momentum once again, that she could prove her electability and quiet the calls for her to quit the race, as well as gaining more support among Democrats and pledged Superdelegates.

Their reasons for continuing were very much the same, however a win in Pennsylvania was perhaps even more critical for Hillary. If she didn't win by a substantial margin, would the calls for her to quit the race get louder? Would she eventually end her campaign or would she continue her vow to fight on until the August convention? A great deal was at stake in Pennsylvania on April 22, 2008. And after Pennsylvania there were still nine more contests, and most polls suggested very tight races. To win, could Barack count on the African American votes in states like North Carolina with 134 delegates, and in West Virginia with 39 delegates at stake? Could Hillary count on Indiana Senator Evan Bayh's support and could she win in Indiana with their 84 delegates? Would voters in Montana and South Dakota—two states with primaries that, historically, hadn't been very important—support Barack or Hillary? And in Kentucky and Oregon on May 20, where both candidates were campaigning, who would win the total of 110 delegates in such demographically different states?

Hillary was well aware of the contests that remained and the long odds she faced, especially if the votes cast in Michigan and Florida did not count. As the Democratic National Convention got closer, it remained to be seen if the continual bickering back and forth between the two candidates and their resulting increasingly negative images in the minds of the voters would hurt the eventual Democratic nominee in the general election against strong Republican candidate John McCain. The speculation would continue until at least the end of the primary season on June 3, 2008, if not until the Democratic National Convention in August.

THE ISSUE OF RACE IN THE 2008 CAMPAIGN

At the Democratic National Convention in July 2004, Barack said, "In no other country on earth is my story even possible." On March 18, 2008, Barack said this again when he talked about his candidacy and the issue of race in America. The race for the 2008 presidency was truly historic; for the first time in the nation's history, a black man and a woman were running for the highest office in the land and to be the leader of the free world. From the moment he entered the race in February 2007, Barack's campaign was likened to a movement. As he traveled around the country, from center stages and town halls, to diners and rallies at arenas, to high school gymnasiums and county fairs, Barack generated excitement in America and around the world. However, race was something that seemed to be seething just beneath the surface.

In the first months of 2008, racial issues rippled through Barack's smooth, confident campaign. Despite his wins in states like Iowa and Wyoming, where there were few African American voters, racial issues entered conversations and permeated the news cycles. Since announcing his candidacy, Barack had been criticized for not being "black enough" and for being "too black"; he had always tried to transcend these questions by concentrating on the issues, by talking to all voters, by being inclusive. And while these questions and criticisms were discussed and written about during the first year of the campaign, by February 2008, racial tensions bubbled up and the race issue gained momentum. To add to the tensions surrounding this important issue were the videotaped snippets of racial rhetoric made by Barack's long-time pastor, the Reverend Jeremiah A. Wright Jr. The video was played over and over on news outlets and on YouTube; it was discussed on talk radio and was written about in newspapers and on political blogs. There were calls for Barack to denounce the pastor and distance himself from him and the church itself. There were calls that questioned patriotism and questions about why Barack hadn't left the church a long time ago.

For Barack, he had always carefully and deliberately avoided the stereotype of being an angry black politician. He had always tried, with much success certainly, as evidenced by his cross-over support in primaries and caucuses, to appeal to all walks of life and all races; he was adamant in his speeches and also in his political career in appealing to all, and he did not want to be stereotyped or pigeonholed. To quell the firestorm caused by his former pastor's fiery racial rhetoric, Barack tried to discuss the issues and stay on his message; he also tried to quietly distance himself from his long-time pastor, the man he called his spiritual leader and the pastor who performed his marriage ceremony and baptized his two daughters. He then, not quietly, but adamantly, denounced Wright's charges about white America, assuring America that he did not agree with it, and called it divisive—but this was not enough. Deciding he needed to address the issue of race and the racial rhetoric displayed by Wright head-on, on March 18, 2008, at the National Constitution Center in Philadelphia, not far from where the Constitution of the United States was written, Barack made what many described as the most important speech on race in America since Dr. Martin Luther King's "I Have a Dream" speech. Speaking for nearly 40 minutes, Barack confronted America's legacy of racial division and white resentment and urged America to overcome "a racial stalemate we've been stuck in for years." Barack said, "We have a choice in this country: we can accept a politics that breeds division, and conflict, and cynicism. Or, at this moment, we can come together and say: 'not this time.'"[25]

In the speech, Barack said once again that in no other country in the world was his story possible, reminding his listeners that he was the son of a white woman from Kansas and a black man from Africa. The speech was made more than a year into a campaign that many felt transcended race, by a man who adamantly intended to build a broad coalition of racial and ethnic groups and who never wanted to be pigeonholed as a black politician. Political pundits were quick to pick apart the speech; some thought the speech was as much about who Barack is as it was about his words. Some thought it was more rhetoric and did not answer questions or say anything new. Still others thought Barack should denounce and disown Wright for his racial, fiery rhetoric. Some thought it was the most important speech made in recent history and one that harkened back to Abraham Lincoln, Martin Luther King, and John F. Kennedy. Some applauded and others were more than skeptical. The question was whether the speech was enough to satisfy voters, or if it just raised more questions. Whether the speech, as bold as it was, and as risky as it may have been for Barack, would help or hurt the Barack Obama campaign remained to be seen, but it was certainly historic and certainly powerful. In his speech, Barack claimed that the success of his own campaign in winning voters from all ethnic and social groups had proved that "America can change."

He added, "And today, whenever I find myself feeling doubtful or cynical about this possibility, what gives me the most hope is the next generation: the young people whose attitude and beliefs and openness to change have already made history in this election."[26]

A POLITICAL MOVEMENT, AN AUDACITY OF HOPE

Generations of Americans have responded with a simple creed that sums up the spirit of a people: Yes, we can.

—*Barack Obama*

It was in November 2006 that Barack Obama first met with friends and advisers to discuss what it would take for him to make a run for the presidency. For many at the meeting, Barack's success at winning the nomination was a long shot, but the prospect of his run created great excitement for sure. As the group weighed such challenges as raising enough money, the toll it would likely take on Barack's family, and the organization that would have to be built, the energy and interest were palpable. Barack was truly a rising star in politics, and his ability to compromise, inspire, and motivate was becoming well known. Few had forgotten his electrifying speech at the Democratic Convention in July 2004. And while he might be a long shot, no one dismissed his ability or his chances to be the nominee for the Democratic Party. In February 2007, he formally announced his bid, after many discussions with the same friends and advisers and with his wife, Michelle. Once he began to campaign, there were fits and starts and bumps in the road, and mistakes. But there were also successes; his eloquence, his commitment and drive, and his motivational speeches gained attention and the momentum began to build.

A year after announcing his candidacy, Barack had a momentum that many speculated could not be stopped. He was ahead in delegate count and in the popular vote. Adam Nagourney wrote in the *New York Times*, on February 13, 2008, "If the election was one where a candidate wins by virtue of being seen as winning, the definition of momentum, it would mean that voters in future primary and caucus contests would be influenced by the outcome of all the earlier contests."[27] Still, Barack was not a shoo-in for the Democratic nomination by beating his rival Hillary Clinton. And whether he could win the presidency against the formidable Senator John McCain, who became the presumptive Republican nominee on March 4, 2008, no one knew. All this remained to be seen, but when Barack took his campaign to Wisconsin for the February 19 primary, he told an estimated crowd of 17,000 cheering supporters, "Tonight we are on our way.

We also know at this moment the cynics can no longer say that our hope is false. We have now won east and west, north and south, and across the heartland of this country we love. We have given young people a reason to believe, and brought folks back to the polls who want to believe again. And we are bringing together Democrats and Independents and Republicans; blacks and whites; Latinos and Asians; small states and big states, and Red States and Blue States, into the United States of America."[28]

Because of Barack Obama, something big has been stirring in American politics; it has meant change and a new direction, an energy few had seen before; it has meant that perhaps there might be a new vision of America around the world, and it has meant an audacity of hope. To many, supporting the Barack Obama campaign meant feeling a patriotism they hadn't felt for a long time or ever before, and it meant supporting a candidate who had the ability to unite Americans and give a new face to America around world. Representative Elijah Cummings may have said it best when he introduced Barack at a rally in Baltimore, Maryland, just before that state's primary. He said, "This is not a campaign for the presidency of the United States. This is a movement."[29]

NOTES

1. Alec MacGillis, "A Margin That Will Be Hard to Marginalize," *Washington Post*, January 27, 2008, A01.

2. Richard Stengel, "Democracy Reborn," *Time*, February 11, 2008, 6.

3. Caroline Kennedy, "A President Like My Father," *New York Times*, January 27, 2008, wk. 18.

4. David Von Drehle, "It's Their Turn Now," *Time*, February 11, 2008.

5. Ibid., 38.

6. Ibid., 37.

7. Ibid., 38.

8. Robin Toner, "High Enthusiasm Propels Democrats," *New York Times*, January 29, 2008, A.1.

9. "Election Guide 2008," *New York Times*, February 13, 2008, http://politics.nytimes.com/election-guide/2008/results/votes/index.html.

10. Ibid.

11. Bob Benenson and Marie Horrigan, "Obama Wins Convincingly in South Carolina, as Rivals Look Ahead," *CQ Today*, January 27, 2008, http://www.cqpolitics.com.

12. Ibid.

13. Patrick Healy, "Obama and Clinton Brace for Long Run," *New York Times*, February 7, 2008, A.1.

14. John Dickerson, "Bragging Rights," *Slate*, February 5, 2008, http://www.slate.com/id/2183819.

15. Joe Klein, "Inspiration vs. Substance," *Time*, February 18, 2008, 17.

16. Kate Zernike and John Sullivan, "Obama Wins Maine, Giving Him 4 Victories in Weekend," *New York Times*, February 10, 2008, A.1.

17. "Election Guide 2008," *New York Times*, February 13, 2008, http://politics.nytimes.com/election-guide/2008/results/votes/index.html.

18. John M. Broder and Dalia Sussman, "Obama and McCain Sweep 3 Primaries," *New York Times*, February 13, 2008, A.1.

19. "Election Guide 2008," *New York Times*, March 18, 2008, http://politics.nytimes.com/election-guide/2008/results/votes/index.html.

20. David Jackson, Kathy Kiely, and Jill Lawrence, "Women, Latino Voters Give Clinton Hope of Slowing Obama's Charge," *USA Today*, March 5, 2008, 5A.

21. Jeff Zeleny, "Obama Seeks to Rally Backers after Clinton Victories," *New York Times*, March 5, 2008, A.18.

22. http://politics.nytimes.com/election-guide/2008/results/superdelegates/index.html (April 4, 2008).

23. John Harwood, "In Superdelegate Count, Tough Math for Clinton," *New York Times.com*, April 7, 2008. http://nytimes.com.

24. Mark Halperin, "Clinton: Don't 'shut this race down,'" *Time*, April 7, 2008, 28.

25. Tom Baldwin, "Barack Obama Attacks US State of 'Racial Stalemate,'" *Times Online*, March 19, 2008, http://www.timesonline.co.uk/tol/news/world/us_and_americas/us_elections/article3578425.ece.

26. Ibid.

27. Adam Nagourney, "Surging, Obama Makes His Case," *New York Times*, February 13, 2008, A.21.

28. Barack Obama, "February 12 Speech," *New York Times*, February 12, 2008, http://nytimes.com/2008/02/12/us/politics.

29. Thomas F. Schaller, "Potomac Pummeling," *American Prospect*, February 13, 2008, http://www.prospect.org/cs/articles?article=potomac_pummeling.

BIBLIOGRAPHY

Alter, Jonathan. "The Challenges We Face." *Newsweek*, December 25, 2006, 36–40.

Alter, Jonathan, and Daren Brisco. "The Audacity of Hope." *Newsweek*, December 27, 2004, 74–87.

———. "Is America Ready?" *Newsweek*, December 25, 2006, 38–35.

Asante, Molefi Kete. "Barack Obama and the Dilemma of Power." *Journal of Black Studies* 48:1 (2007): 105–115.

Astill, James. "The Campaign's Brightest Star." *The Economist*, June 16, 2007, 33.

Balz, Dan. "With Campaign Underway, Obama Now Must Show More Than Potential." *Washington Post*, February 13, 2007, A9.

Borger, Gloria. "Does Barack Really Rock?" *U.S. News & World Report*, November 6, 2006, 43.

Briscoe, Daren. "Black and White." *Newsweek*, July 8, 2007.

Broder, John M. "Shushing the Baby Boomers." *New York Times*, January 21, 2007, 1, 14.

Brooks, David. "The Obama-Clinton Issue." *New York Times*, December 18, 2007.

———. "The Two Earthquakes." *New York Times*, January 4, 2008.

Brozyna, Christine. "Get to Know Barack Obama." *ABC News Online*, November 1, 2007. http://www.abcnews.com.

Bryant, Nick. "A Black Man in the White House?" *BBC News*, July 3, 2007. http://news.bbc.co.uk.

Butterfield, Fox. "First Black Elected to Head Harvard's Law Review." *New York Times*, February 6, 1990, A20.

Calmes, Jackie. "Democrats' Litmus: Electability: Key Issue for 2008 Race Poses Hurdles for Clinton, Obama." *Wall Street Journal*, January 11, 2007, A6.

Clayton, Jonathan, and Nyangoma Kogela. "Favourite Son Is Already a Winner in Kenya." *Times of London*, February 10, 2007.

Clayworth, Jason. "Obama Victory Speech: 'Time for Change Has Come.'" *Des Moines Register*, January 4, 2008.

Davey, Monica. "As Quickly as Overnight, a Democratic Star Is Born." *New York Times*, March 18, 2004, A20.

Devaney, Sherri, and Mark Devaney. *Barack Obama*. Farmington Hills, MI: Thompson Gale, 2007.

Drew, Christopher, and Mike McIntire. "Obama Built Donor Network from Roots Up." *New York Times*, April 3, 2007.

Duffy, Michael. "Obama Moves on, without a Bounce." *Time*, January 9, 2008.

Enda, Jodi. "Great Expectations." *American Prospect Online*, February 5, 2006. http://www.prospect.org.

Ferguson, Andrew. "The Literary Obama." *Weekly Standard*, February 12, 2007.

Foulkes, Toni. "Case Study: Chicago—The Barack Obama Campaign." *Social Policy* Winter 2003, Vol. 34, No. 2 and Spring 2004, Vol. 34, No. 3: 49–51.

Gensheimer, Lydia. "Big Crowd, Big Win for Obama in Heart of Des Moines." *CQ Today*, January 4, 2008.

Giroux, Greg. "Obama and Huckabee Score Upsets in Iowa." *CQ Today*, January 4, 2008.

Green, David. "Candidacy Status: Sen. Barack Obama (IL)." *National Public Radio*, July 9, 2007. http://www.npr.org.

Greenberg, David. "How Obama Is Like JFK." *Washington Post*, April 20, 2007.

Grim, Ryan. "Obama's World." *The Politico*, March 6, 2007. http://www.cbsnews.com.

Healy, Patrick. "Obama Woos Key Blacks." *Denver Post*, April 22, 2007.

Ifill, Gwen. "On the Road with Michelle." *Essence*, September 2007, 203–206.

Kantor, Jodi. "In Law School, Obama Found Political Voice." *New York Times*, January 28, 2007, 1, 21.

———. "A Candidate, His Minister and the Search for Faith." *New York Times*, April 30, 2007.

Kaufman, Jonathan. "Whites' Great Hope?" *Wall Street Journal*, November 10, 2007, A1.

Keen, Judy. "Candid and Unscripted, Campaigning Her Way." *USA Today*, May 11, 2007.

Klein, Joe. "The Fresh Face." *Time*, October 23, 2006, 44.

———. "How to Build a Bonfire." *Time*, February 26, 2007, 18.

———. "Barack Obama." *Time*, May 14, 2007, 57–58.

————. "Obama's Historic Victory." *Time*, January 4, 2008. http://www.time.com/time/politics/article/0,8599,1700132,00.html.

La Ganga, Maria L. "Obama Has New Rallying Cry: Yes, We Can!" *Los Angeles Times*, January 9, 2008.

Little, Amanda Griscom. "Barack Obama." *Rolling Stone*, December 30, 2004, 88.

Lizza, Ryan. "The Natural." *Atlantic Monthly*, September 2004, 30–33.

MacFarquhar, Larissa. "The Conciliator." *The New Yorker*, May 7, 2007.

————. "Ask the Author: 'The Conciliator.'" *The New Yorker*, May 14, 2007.

Marcus, Ruth. "The Clintonian Candidate." *Washington Post*, January 31, 2007, A15.

Mendell, David. *Obama: From Promise to Power*. New York: Amistad, 2007.

Merida, Kevin. "The Ghost of a Father." *Washington Post*, December 14, 2007, A12.

Merrion, Paul. "Obama's Appeal Drives Cash Flow." *Paul Crain's Chicago Business*, September 15, 2003.

Moberg, David. "Obama's Community Roots." *The Nation*, April 3, 2007.

Mosk, Matthew, and John Solomon. "Obama Taps Two Worlds to Fill 2008 War Chest." *Washington Post*, April 15, 2007, A1.

Mundy, Liza. "A Series of Fortunate Events." *Washington Post*, August 12, 2007, W10.

Nagourney, Adam, and Jeff Zeleny. "Obama Formally Enters Presidential Race with Calls for Generational Change." *New York Times*, February 11, 2007, 22.

Noonan, Peggy. "Declarations: 'The Man from Nowhere.'" *Wall Street Journal*, December 16, 2006, 14.

Norment, Lynn. "The Hottest Couple in America." *Ebony*, February 1, 2007.

Obama, Barack. *Dreams from My Father*. New York: Three Rivers Press, 2004.

————. *The Audacity of Hope*. New York: Crown Publishers, 2006.

————. "Presidential Exploratory Committee." *Barack Obama Home Page*. http://www.barackobama.com.

————. "Renewing American Leadership." *Foreign Affairs*, July/August 2007.

————. "Major Speech on Iraq." *Barack Obama Home Page*. http://www.barackobama.com.

————. "On the Issues." *Barack Obama Home Page*. http://www.barackobama.com.

————. "Caucus Speech." *New York Times*, January 3, 2008.

————. "Concession Speech." http://thepage.time.com.

"Obama Well-Traveled in Brief Senate Career." *CNN.com*, February 2, 2007. http://www.cnn.com/2007/politics/02/15.

"Obamamania." *The Economist*, October 28, 2006, 42.

"Obama's Second Coming." *The Economist*, November 6, 2004, 33.

Page, Susan. "2008 Race Has the Face of a Changing America." *USA Today*, March 12, 2007.

Pelofsky, Jeremy. "Sen. Obama Nears Clinton in Campaign Money Race." *Reuters*, April 4, 2007.

Pindell, James. "The Obama Factor." *Campaigns & Elections*, December 2006, 98.

Pitney, John J. Jr. "George W. Obama." *National Review Online*, February 28, 2007, http://www.nationalreview.com.

Quindlen, Anna. "A Leap into the Possible." *Newsweek*, August 9, 2004, 60.

Ripley, Amanda, David Thigpen, and Jeannie McCabe. "Obama's Ascent." *Time*, November 15, 2004, 74–81.

Roach, Ronald. "Obama Rising." *Black Issues in Higher Education* 21:17 (2004): 20–23.

Robinson, Eugene. "The Moment for this Messenger?" *Washington Post*, March 13, 2007, A17.

Rudin, Ken. "Obama, or a History of Black Presidents of the U.S." *National Public Radio*, December 7, 2006. http://www.npr.org.

Schaller, Thomas F. "Potomac Pummeling," *American Prospect*, February 13, 2008.

Scharnberg, Kirsten, and Kim Barker. "The Not-So-Simple Story of Barack Obama's Youth." *Chicago Tribune*, March 25, 2007.

Scheiber, Noam. "Race against History." *New Republic* 230:20 (2004): 21–26.

Scott, Janney. "In Illinois, Obama Proved Pragmatic and Shrewd." *New York Times*, July 30, 2007.

———. "In 2000, a Streetwise Veteran Schooled a Bold Young Obama." *New York Times*, September 9, 2007.

———. "Memories of Obama in New York Differ." *New York Times*, October 29, 2007.

"Secret Service to Watch Obama; Racism a Concern." *USA Today*, May 3, 2007.

Silverstein, Ken. "Barack Obama Inc." *Harper's Magazine*, November 2006, 31–40.

Slevin, Peter. "Obama Forged Political Mettle in Illinois Capitol." *Washington Post*, February 9, 2007, A1.

Spencer, Jim. "Obama Needs Inspiration to Get His Optimism Across." *Denver Post*, March 19, 2007.

Szep, Jason, and Ellen Wulfhorst. "Undecided Voters Give Obama Hope in 2008 Race." *Reuters*, November 21, 2007.

Toomey, Shamus. "A Lot to Do with Race." *Chicago Sun Times*, May 5, 2007.

"The Triumph of Hope over Experience." *The Economist*, December 15, 2007, 16–17.

Victor, Kirk. "In His Own Words." *National Journal*, March 18, 2006, 22–23.

Wallace-Wells, Benjamin. "The Great Black Hope." *Washington Monthly*, November 2004, 30–36.

————. "Obama's Narrator." *New York Times Magazine*, April 1, 2007, 30–35.

Walsh, Kenneth T. "Talkin' 'Bout My New Generation." *U.S. News & World Report*, January 8, 2007, 26–28.

"Where's the Beef?" *The Economist*, April 14, 2007, 36.

Wolfe, Richard, and Daren Briscoe. "Across the Divide." *Newsweek*, July 16, 2007, 22–30, 34.

York, Byron. "Obama Madness." *National Review*, November 20, 2006, 17–18.

Younge, Gary. "The Obama Effect." *The Nation*, December 31, 2007.

Zeleny, Jeff. "As Candidate, Obama Carves Antiwar Stance." *New York Times*, February 26, 2007.

INDEX

About the Author

JOANN F. PRICE is a writing coach and author of *Martha Stewart: A Biography* (Greenwood, 2007).